C000027256

IMAGES
of Sport

BRISTOL
FOOTBALL CLUB (RFU)
1945-2001

To George

With thanks and best wishes

Dave Fox

A fascinating group of past and present rugby greats shown together at a Cleve Rugby Club dinner in the 1960s. On the left stands Bristol's great pre-war fly-half Jimmy Barrington. Next to him are broadcaster G.V. Wynne-Jones, former Gloucester forward 'Bumps' Carpenter and Bristol's greatest pre-war forward Sam Tucker. Next to Tucker is Don Burland, Bristol's England centre of the 1930s. The group is completed by Welsh international, British Lion and wartime member of Bristol Supporters team Jack Matthews and John Thorne, Bristol's England hooker of 1963.

IMAGES
of Sport

BRISTOL
FOOTBALL CLUB (RFU)
1945-2001

Compiled by
Dave Fox & Mark Hoskins

TEMPUS

First published 2001
Copyright © Dave Fox and Mark Hoskins, 2001

Tempus Publishing Limited
The Mill, Brimscombe Port,
Stroud, Gloucestershire, GL5 2QG

ISBN 0 7524 2410 6

Typesetting and origination by
Tempus Publishing Limited
Printed in Great Britain by
Midway Colour Print, Wiltshire

Acknowledgements

Producing a book like this is great fun, but hard work. Our first volume on Bristol, covering the first fifty-odd years, received great support from the former players of the club and their families. When the response from those that matter is so good, you know it's worth the effort. We hope this book will do justice to the players and officials of more recent years. Once again, we are grateful to Tempus for giving us the chance to produce this book. We now have the bit between our teeth and we hope to write further publications on Bristol in the future.

For invaluable assistance with this edition, we would particularly like to thank Gordon Lovell, the secretary of Bristol Rugby Former Players, for his help with making contacts and opening doors for us. We would also like to thank Gordon Allen, Brian Amesbury, Timothy Auty, Ian Bell, Bob and Fran Bennett, Andy Blackmore, Christine Blake, Ron Bridgeman, John Broad, John Carr, Richard Cecil, Treve Chesterfield, Ken Coggins, Peter Colston, Phil Davidge, Robert Davies, Allan Dutton, Mike Ellery, Geoff Farley, David Foot, Pete Francomb and the staff of SPP Publishing, George Gallop, George Gibbs, Connie Goulstone, George Green, Derek Griffiths, Alan Hale, John Harding, Lionel and Sylvia Harvey, Dick Hawkes, John Hellings, Meric Hill, Steve Hill, Peter Hillard, Doreen Hussey, John Kelland, Wynne Jones, Jeff Kemp, Bert Macdonald, John Mace, Tom Mahoney, Alan Morley, Chris Nash, Derek Neate, Julie Nicholson, Alan Pearn, David Perkins, Jean Pratten, Nigel Pomphrey, Mike Rafter, Bill Redwood, Arthur Sheppard, John Thorne, Ron Trott, Geoff Tucker, George Tucker, John Watson, Peter Watts, Bill Webley, David Weeks, Chris Williams, John Williams and the staff of the Bristol Record Office, Neil Williams, Sheila Williams, Chris Woodward, David Woodward, the staff of the *Bristol Evening Post*, the management of Bristol Shoguns (as the club is now called), and Ray Ruddick and Bunty for their encouragement and assistance with collation, administration and commas. We would also, of course, like to thank John Mason, the perceptive and articulate former rugby correspondent of the *Bristol Evening Post* and, latterly, *The Daily Telegraph*, for his thought-provoking introduction. We don't believe we have contravened any copyright – if we have, then we apologise.

As with our previous volume, this book is about the players, for without them there wouldn't be a Bristol club. They are a very special group of people who have entertained so many for so long. This book is once more dedicated to them all, but we would like especially to mention George Gibbs and John Broad, both of whom died whilst we were compiling the book.

Dave Fox and Mark Hoskins
Bristol, October 2001

Contents

Foreword
No Bounds For Alpha Plus Bristol

In being invited to offer a few post-Second World War thoughts on the Bristol club, past and present, I'm flattered. Plainly residence in Sea Mills as a lad and, thereafter, as a semi-itinerant around the city, be it Stoke Bishop, Stapleton, Knowle, Clifton, Westbury Park or, finally, Frenchay, cannot be sufficient qualification. The clue must lie with my first employers after leaving Colston's School, Stapleton, armed with the History Prize and a Bristol University School Certificate in seven subjects. Yes, the *Bristol Evening Post*, not for the first time, bless them, have much for which to answer. Talk about leaps in the dark!

To the distant (mostly loyal) Bristol supporter – I left the fair city more than thirty years ago for Surrey's urban glades and have lived there ever since – the club's attitudes and endeavours, the style, the polish, have a special affection. It has been a devotion which began in early teenage when at Colston's, in those days a boarders-only grim edifice at the top of Bell Hill. Then, in term time, it was not permissible to turn left out of those impressive dolphin-ornate high-rise green gates.

It matters not a jot that the rugby bond, subsequently, became professional. Until being recruited by *The Daily Telegraph* in 1968, I had been in the privileged position, for six tumultuous seasons, of reporting Bristol's activities on and off the field for the *Evening Post*. Somerset cricket, too. After fourteen years as a general news reporter and feature writer in Bristol and London, a career change of direction led me into sports journalism. Could this, I wonder, have been the late reward for schoolboy boldness? After all, were Bristol not the club I had broken school bounds to watch?; the club that later prompted the real risk of being labelled absent without leave from my army unit?; the club that, ultimately, shaped my ideas about the game?; about how rugby union should be played and what needed to be done to succeed at the highest level? Simply, yes.

The compelling memory of Bristol rugby, especially so when closely involved in the 1960s, has to be a combination of power, pace, and perception. The club were playing an all-running, all-handling form of the game long, long before it became the laudable fashion in the southern hemisphere. And often on a mud-heap, too, certainly until Spring had sprung.

The late John Blake, a man of vision and sincerity, sheepishly admitted at an early point that no matter what the coaching manuals had to say about the duties of an outside-half, he had to play ball in hand. 'Got no choice', the Blake chin slightly raised, eyes twinkling, he told me: 'I can't kick. Anyway I'm a failed scrum-half'.

The irony of Bristol's more recent trials and tribulations, of which I know little, is that until, say, a dozen years ago, they were an acknowledged power in the land; even Bath were respectful. I have never been one for a pile of statistics, for example: Side A win 62 per cent possession, tight and loose. Where, though, was that ball won?; what was done with that possession? Then, too often, the biter bit, the body blow – how was it what Side B won?

But statistician or not, Bristol's records in the forty or so post-war seasons before leagues started (1987) do indicate that the club had their moments. Hundreds of them. At random, I offer the following: 7 defeats in 1955/56; barely 30 losses in 170-plus matches, 1955-59. There were 38 wins in 1966/67. Mind you, Bristol did play 55 matches that season – and if Derek Neate had had his way, he would have played in every one.

Mike Ellery, a contemporary of mine at Colston's where, believe it or not, he was not regarded as rugby player, re-wrote the club's try-scoring records in this period: 251 in 347 matches. Then along came another Colstonian by the name of Morley. I took him on his first overseas rugby tour and came back from Italy convinced that here was a special (rugby) talent. I dared to say so early on in a *Telegraph* column. Noisy, cheerful Alan, bless him, did not let me down: 384 tries for Bristol in 520 games and (I think) a career-total 479, a union world record. Yes, I'm glad I broke boarding school bounds those years ago. But then, I'm totally biased.

Admittedly, mind you, when swept up in Bristol's warm rugby embrace (professionally and personally), there was often more than a touch of the bizarre in matches that could lurch from the mundane to the marvellous (and back again) in the blink of an eyelid. The clattering defence of opponents may have kept the lid on the Bristol pot for the first twenty minutes or so, but with the kitchen growing hotter and hotter, the simmering could reach boiling point well before half-time.

What were the virtues sought by a succession of Bristol captains: Blake, Neate, Peter Colston, Bill Redwood, Dick Hawkes and, probably, the best of them all, Bert Macdonald? As ever, hard, unflinching work up front and, when called for, rapid possession. Thereafter the backs took charge: the timing of the pass, the strength to stand up in the tackle, the availability of the ball before, during and after the tackle, and, best of all, vision, the awareness of what was happening around them. In two words – unit skills.

The willingness to invent, to improvise, carried risk, of course. The opposition lying up as close as they dared – and further, if the referee was lost in admiration – seizing upon the rare dropped ball. The belief that counter-attack from deep was admirable – that run out of defence was, at best, ambitious, bold even. Dangerous, too. I remember Newport sneaking a win when Bristol's boldness came unstuck. Yes, and others, of course. Nothing run-of-the-mill about BRIS, I'll have you know.

Yes, Bristol did pay the price of defeat at times, despite having made all the running. Helter-skelter movement, not always coherent, was a robust facet of Bristol rugby, laced with the unpredictable – as demonstrated amply in my time by the Redwoods (Bill in particular; Pop Percy too), Roy Dash, Len Davies, Malcolm Lewis. Invariably, the player who brought a calming touch to the proceedings: Jim Glover, hugely unsung, hugely influential in Bristol's midfield, all of which was done with a healthy helping of competitive chivalry.

Without indulging in a laundry list of names it is well-nigh impossible, even briefly, to do justice to Bristol's best. The goal-kickers, for instance: Bob Challis, Alan Pearn and, perhaps, top of the tree, Gordon Cripps, 1951-62 (11 seasons) 1,310 points overall, 1,765 to include United matches. Gordon was a lock forward of wiry power and remarkable stamina at a time when fitness was more miss than hit. Forward strength, as we all know, even backs, is an essential ingredient for success. Who better then, than John Pullin, a Lion, an England captain, Mr Modesty personified, Big Dave Watt, the consistent John Currie, much underrated, as, later on, were Ralph Knibbs, Phil Cue and Mark Tainton.

So, too, were Eric Blackman, who now proudly, deservedly, sports the RFU badge and a host of administrative responsibilities nationwide, Mike Lawrence, Kevin Bogira, Pete Polledri, Nigel Pomphrey, David Sorrell. Paeans of praise also for John Thorne, England tie at the high port (January 1963), Mike Rafter, the grafter, Dave Rollitt, the greying fox, and a man it was a privilege to have known: Doug Pratten. Nor must I ignore those flighty gents behind the scrum – Terry Base, Richard Harding, Mike Collins, David Weeks, Peter Knight and, further back, Vic Thompson and Jack Gregory, an Olympic sprinter.

Tom Mahoney requires a chapter to himself. So do Percy Redwood and Ronnie Morris – and if Spud Murphy was still about, he'd make certain he got two chapters. How on earth dare I omit Dave Tyler, he of the flaring nostrils, or Fred Williams, super prop, or John Scott, a ball-carrying forward equally at home in the front or back rows, or, come to that, David Hazell or Bev Dovey, schoolmasters both, gnarled props both?

My abject apologies should your favourite Bristol player have been left out, be they Richard Wallace, Keith Smith or Ron Bridgeman or Laurie Watts or Jack Dalziel or Denzil Golledge or George Gibbs or Roy Muller or George Green or Fred Hill or Basil Griffin. Do I hear plaudits, too, for Barry Nelmes, Bob Hesford, Charlie Hannaford, Dave Impey, the thinking man's hooker, and Neil Mayne, sporting his Bristol tie in distant parts of the world? Good host, too, I recollect on one of my 1,001 overseas trips carrying the *Telegraph* banner. The things I did for my readers! The sacrifices! Well, someone had to do it.

Stop, stop, stop. Please remember the only fact about a match is the result; everything else is opinion. Equally, I believe it's an empty exercise attempting to judge the values of players of different generations. Richard Sharp and Tony Nicholls, for instance, would have succeeded in the twenties; similarly Len Corbett, Sam Tucker, too, would have succeeded in the sixties ... in my view.

As, in retirement, I no longer have the public platform I strutted upon for eighteen years as the *Telegraph*'s Chief Rugby Writer, a couple of personal observations in conclusion. Forget for a moment the gales of change that have swept rugby union of late. Ignore, please, the headlong gallop into the seductive embrace of Mammon from more austere traditional concepts of a sport which, from head to toe, Victorian ideals to the fore, proudly presented itself as the leisure pursuit of amateurs, awash with ethos and ethics. Marvellously summed up by an All Black, I recall. 'Too many sweatbands', sniffed Colin 'Pinetree' Meads, when his opinion of British rugby was sought. 'Not enough sweat.'

The good news is that England, like Bristol of old, do have the armoury. The bad news is that not everyone always knows, like Bristol of old, where to find the key. Adaptation, flexibility and the sheer bloody-minded determination to win have not been English characteristics. But for a decade or more Bristol, their lettered jerseys offering a form of dazzling Scrabble, got close. Mighty close.

In the current scene, Rugby union's uncertain advance to a professional game, rewarding contracts and, bless them, business class travel, for the men who make the turnstiles click, is not a fleeting affair. It must become a marriage of substance and for the greater good. Amateurism, a wholly laudable concept, will continue to flourish at levels way beyond the grass roots. At the top end, good riddance to hypocrisy, the brown envelopes and spurious promises, absurd demands on (ostensibly) the then amateur players. Amateurs only in the sense that many were, in effect, paid by either understanding or generous employers – to play rugby. Those days have gone and, in my book, not soon enough. In the shop window of the international arena there are different values: not better or worse, merely different. They always were.

No matter the upheavals in England, the rumblings in Wales, the spits in Scotland, the rivalries in Ireland, 98 per cent of the game, if not more, will stay much as it has been, nationwide leagues notwithstanding: a cheerful haven of limited ambition for the most part, of playing to get or to keep fit, an activity in which the result beforehand is of prime importance and of little consequence afterwards, once the first couple of pints have been supped.

A final Bristol thought, if not also upon the game which has been, family apart (thank you, Agnes and Susan) the cornerstone of my life. When it comes to the roller-coaster of game-playing emotions, the fascinating battle of mind and muscle, rapier and claymore, in exploring the unbridled joy of victory against all odds, the depths of sporting despair at unexpected defeat, Bristol would, in my day, have won a fairground of prizes.

So, for this one-time very junior reporter, it's Bristol unbounded, so to speak, with apologies to Colston's and Maestro Foster, the housemaster who spotted me on a return journey from the Memorial Ground to Stapleton. I was gated for weeks, shorn of all privileges, such as they were. Never should have run after that bus.

Little did I appreciate that a dozen years later, off and on the field Roger Grove or Mike Pegler, or Watty or 'Polly' Perkins to the fore, a more friendly, co-operative group of young men in the public eye would have been difficult to find. They invariably offered the three E's: Entertainment, Excitement, Enjoyment.

In truth, though, the best E of all was Excellence, all which adds up in my (biased) opinion to A for Alpha, if not Alpha Plus. John Broad, bless him, thought so – and it never was wise to argue with him. Even if you dared to take such a course, there was always the broad Broad smile in return. He knew best: Alpha Plus, without doubt.

John Mason,
Hampton Wick, Surrey
October 2001

One

Renaissance

1945-1953

As the Second World War drew to a close, the Bristol club was relaunched, in May 1945, and the first official fixture was against Stroud the following September, Bristol winning 21-3. The game was preceded by the rededication of the Memorial Ground by the Lord Mayor, the ground thus becoming a memorial to local rugby players who died in the two world wars. A service was held on the pitch, prior to the kick-off of this historic match. The 1945/46 team is from left to right, back row: G. Hogarth, A.J. Owens Britton (secretary), P.J. Down (chairman), G.G. Babbage (treasurer), C.R. Murphy. Middle row: E.E. McCall, G.E. Green, G.S. Priddle, J.E. Harris, F.C. Hill, E.E. Houlden, J. Priest. Front row: D.G. Pratten, G.H. Houlden, L.J. Griffin, V.H. Thompson (captain), T.A.B. Mahoney, R.R. Morris, T.H. Griffiths.

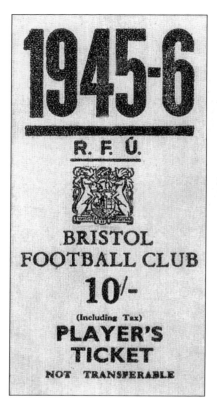

1945-6

R. F. U.

BRISTOL
FOOTBALL CLUB
10/-
(Including Tax)
PLAYER'S
TICKET
NOT TRANSFERABLE

The final record for the 1945/46 season was not outstanding, with defeats outnumbering victories, but the return of regular rugby was a joy and a relief to many. The fixture list was much as it had been in 1939, with the addition of one-off fixtures against New Zealand Services and the Royal Australian Air Force. The team members included pre-war stalwarts such as Tom Mahoney and Charlie Murphy, as well as Jack Harris, who, uniquely, played for the club under two surnames. He played initially as Horton, but was adopted at the age of twenty-one and took his new family's surname. This illustration shows a 1945/6 player's ticket.

Thanks to the efforts of the Bristol Supporters' team, the rugby flame had been kept alight in the city during the war and members of this team provided the backbone of the 1945/46 side. Full-back V.H. Thompson had captained the supporters and was the obvious choice as Bristol's first post-war captain. Vic Thompson, one of a line of Colston's School full-backs to play for the club, made his first appearance in 1937 and played 91 games in all. He also played for Somerset, before a broken leg during the Neath game of 1947 ended his career. Thompson, who died in 1999, was a farmer at Publow, Pensford, in Somerset. His son, Bruce, also played full-back for Bristol.

Winger G.E. Green, a first lieutenant in the Royal Navy during the war, played occasional games for the Bristol Supporters' team. He was reserve to attend Bristol's first post-war fixture and was waiting at the entrance to the ground just before kick-off, when Vic Thompson approached and told him to report to the dressing rooms as another player, Syd Wheatley, was unable to play. He managed to join the team just in time for the kick-off. George Green enjoyed an impressive debut, scoring a hat-trick of tries. He went on to play 118 first-team games, scoring a total of 53 tries. Not so lucky was left-wing Ralph Ralph, also making his debut. Ralph, a noted local cricketer, was injured after twenty minutes and never played rugby again.

Official Programme 3d.

RUGBY FOOTBALL

Richmond Athletic Ground
E. de LISSA. Secretary.

Richmond & Blackheath

versus

BRISTOL

ON

Saturday, February 16th, 1946

Kick-off 3.0 p.m.

J. H. Broad & Co., Ltd., Printers, 8, King Street, Richmond, Surrey.

Other senior rugby clubs had greater difficulties than Bristol in restarting after the war. London clubs Richmond and Blackheath decided to combine for the 1945/46 season, as Blackheath's ground had suffered war damage and playing strength was low. Bristol played this unique combined team in February 1946, losing 8-6. This is the programme for the match

11

Haydn Tanner first sprang to fame as Swansea's schoolboy scrum-half, when they defeated the 1935 New Zealand All Blacks. He went on to pursue a distinguished career and is recognized as one of Wales's greatest ever scrum-halves. He gained 25 Welsh caps, despite losing some of his best years to the war, and played for the 1938 British Lions in South Africa. He was, briefly, a teacher at Bristol Grammar School and he played twice for Bristol during 1945/46, away against Harlequins and at home against Coventry.

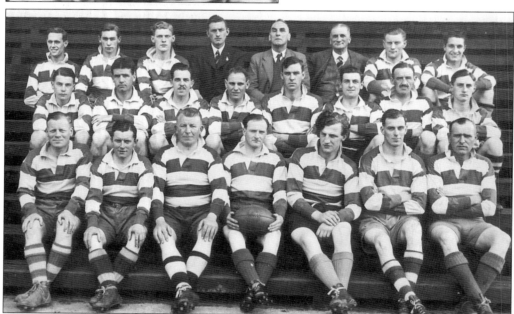

Bristol's Second XV, known as Bristol United since 1929, was called Bristol A XV for the 1945/46 season. This team played local and services sides including RN Barracks Corsham, RAF Colerne, BAC (Bristol Aeroplane Company), Bristol Public and Grammar Schools, and a Forces on Leave XV. Bristol United restarted the following year with a more representative fixture list. From left to right, back row: F. Lowry, G.E. Murphy, M.A. Stephens, L.G. Burland, P.J. Down (chairman), G.G. Babbage (treasurer), D. Home, A. Dutton. Middle row: A. Stone, A. Duggan, W. Vernon, C.W. Webley, J. Clapp, B.E. Wall, A. Rose, T.K. Barrett. Front row: B.E. Clarke, R.R. Morris, N.W. Long, J.R.E. Bryan (captain), R.N. Clarke, D.G. Golledge, J.E. Young.

At the start of the 1946/47 season, Bristol celebrated the twenty-fifth anniversary of the opening of the Memorial Ground. A special fixture was arranged with Cardiff, Bristol's original opponents when the ground opened. Bristol won on that first occasion, but not this time. Cardiff were an outstanding side during the late 1940s, and they won the match 24-0. This was Haydn Tanner's first match for Cardiff and he celebrated with a try, despite the attentions of eighteen-year-old Bristol flanker Allan Dutton, who was draped around his knees as he hurled himself over in the corner. As this was a special fixture, it did not count in the official records of either club but was, nevertheless, a memorable occasion. This is the special souvenir programme.

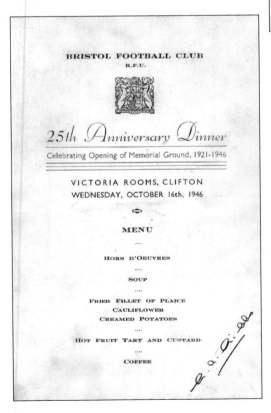

Bristol held two dinners to celebrate the Silver Jubilee of the ground, one at the Grand Hotel in September and the other, following the Cardiff game, at the Victoria Rooms in Clifton. This is the menu for the latter dinner, autographed by future Bristol international George Gibbs. Cardiff's captain for the day, Welsh international Bleddyn Williams, made a speech during which he claimed that Cardiff not only won the game, but beat Bristol at singing as well!

F.C. Hill was Bristol's first post-war hooker, playing 141 games up to 1950. Despite the loss of an eye in a skating accident when he was eighteen, he was highly regarded as a player and was picked by England for two of the Victory Internationals of 1946. These games were not considered full internationals and caps were not awarded. Fred Hill, a carpenter, later played for Bath. His son, Harvey, also hooked for Bristol. Fred Hill died in 1997.

Alun Meredith was Bristol's captain during 1946/47. A student at Bristol University, he only played 42 games for the club, but went on to gain 3 Welsh caps as a member of the Devonport Services team in 1949. A forward, Alun Meredith played county rugby for Devon, Gloucestershire and Yorkshire, and was a director of sport in the Royal Navy.

The harsh winter of 1947 saw the cancellation of many matches and Bristol were out of action for two months. This remarkable photograph is of Bristol's first game after the break, at home to United Services Portsmouth on 15 March. The Memorial Ground is covered in snow, a ghostly crowd huddles under the shed, and a lone figure strides across the terraces, near where the clubhouse now stands. Bristol won this game 16-5.

Alun Meredith's 1946/47 team enjoyed a better record than its immediate predecessor, winning 21 games, drawing 2 and losing 12. Highlights included two wins against Harlequins, and four wins in five days over the Easter period. From left to right, back row: G.A. Gibbs, L. King, V.H. Thompson, G. Hogarth. Third row: P.J. Williams, D.C. Bendall, J.J. Watkins, A.J. Owens Britton (secretary), G.G. Babbage (treasurer), R. Pearce, G.H. Tucker, C.M. Meredith, P.J. Down (chairman). Second row: T.A.B. Mahoney, L.J. Griffin, N. Gibbs, A. Meredith (captain), F.C. Hill, G.E. Green, D. Dobson, D.G. Pratten. Front row: P.D. Sullivan, E.C. Thomas.

G.A. Gibbs, a tank commander in India during the war, was appointed captain for the 1947/48 season and held this office for three seasons in all. He had learnt his rugby at Clifton College, and made his first-team debut in 1939. In 1947, he became Bristol's first post-war international, and he gained a further England cap the following season. A prop forward, George Gibbs also played for Gloucestershire and the Barbarians. He worked for Imperial Tobacco and had to leave Bristol when he was moved by his firm to Newcastle, although he made a brief reappearance in 1953. He later played for Northern and Northumberland. George Gibbs died in 2001.

Nigel Gibbs, a full-back, made his Bristol debut in 1946. Like his brother, George, he was a pupil at Clifton College. He then went to Worcester College, Oxford, and served in submarines during the war. After the war, he became a teacher and eventually moved away from Bristol. He gained both of his England caps in 1954, whilst a member of Harlequins. In 1965, he returned to Bristol as headmaster of Colston's School.

This action shot from October 1947 shows George Green about to score against Bath. Despite Bath's recent dominance in this fixture, Bristol victories still outnumber Bath's by about two to one. On this occasion, Bristol won 26-0.

Another action shot from the same match, this time showing Bristol's other winger, G.H. Tucker, making a break. George Tucker played 85 games for Bristol from 1945 to 1950, scoring 29 tries. A former Imperial player, he first played for Bristol United in the 1938/39 season. He served in the army during the war and joined Bristol when the hostilities were over. He played for Old Redcliffians after leaving Bristol, and later worked with George Gibbs at W.D. & H.O. Wills.

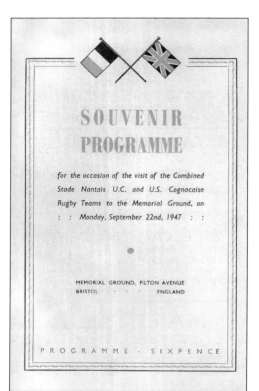

SOUVENIR
PROGRAMME

for the occasion of the visit of the Combined
Stade Nantais U.C. and U.S. Cognacaise
Rugby Teams to the Memorial Ground, on
: : Monday, September 22nd, 1947 : :

MEMORIAL GROUND, FILTON AVENUE
BRISTOL · · · ENGLAND

P R O G R A M M E - S I X P E N C E

Bristol established a playing link with French club Cognac in the 1920s, but were unable to continue this liaison when the RFU suspended all fixtures with French teams in 1931, amidst allegations of widespread professionalism in French club rugby. This ban was lifted in 1939, but the war intervened, so Bristol were particularly delighted to welcome a combined Nantes and Cognac side in 1947 – their first French contact for twenty years. This special souvenir programme was produced for the game, which was won 13-4 by Bristol.

In November 1947, Bristol travelled to France for a return fixture with Nantes, flying to a game for the first time in the club's history. On the outward journey, a small plane carrying five of the party was diverted to Paris, and some panic was caused back home when the plane was reported missing. The *Bristol Evening Post* carried the front-page headline 'Rugby Men Lost'. Blissfully unaware of this, the five passengers spent a happy night at the Folies Bergères, and flew on to Nantes the following day, arriving just in time for the match. This picture shows the team group, prior to the flight.

Bristol's visit coincided with Armistice Day, and Bristol captain George Gibbs marked the occasion by placing a wreath at the Nantes war memorial. He is shown here, watched by his team-mates and representatives from Nantes.

Bristol defeated Nantes 14-3, despite losing George Tucker through injury. No replacements were allowed during a game in those days. The game was billed as 'Grand Match International de Rugby' in the official programme. This photograph shows the Bristol team.

This photograph shows action from the Nantes game. Bristol full-back Meric Hill kicks ahead, with George Green following. Meric Hill, who attended Cotham Grammar School and played for Old Cothamians on either side of the war, made 77 appearances for Bristol and scored 186 points, mainly from kicks. He also played for Somerset and joined the Imperial Club when he left Bristol.

The mayor of Nantes hosted a reception after the game. There was also a visit to an aircraft factory during the trip. Here, a group of players admire a model.

1947/48 was a busy season. In addition to the French trip, there was a three-match tour to Devon and Cornwall in January 1948. Bristol played three games in four days, defeating Plymouth Albion 15-7, Penzance and Newlyn 3-0, and Redruth 6-3. Captain George Gibbs was unable to travel. He had been selected to play for England against the touring Australians, although he subsequently withdrew from the team with an injury. This photograph shows Bristol's tourists outside the Marine Hotel in Penzance. George Hogarth displays a 'Ladies Only' sign – no doubt a tour trophy!

The Bristol Schools' Rugby Union was formed in 1898 and has always enjoyed close links with the Bristol club. Over the years, numerous players have graduated from the Bristol Schools' XV to the senior side. This photograph shows the Bristol Schoolboys' team of 1947, which lost 13-6 to its Gloucester counterparts. In the front row, third from the left, is Arthur Sheppard, an England Schools' international and later a regular in the Bristol pack. On the extreme right of the back row stands the great John Blake, Bristol's influential and innovative captain of the late 1950s.

This picture is included to show the close camaraderie which existed between the Bristol players of this era. It shows the wedding of George Green and Mary Saunders at Emmanuel church, Clifton, on 23 December 1947. Best man, George Gibbs, shakes the groom's hand, watched by Tom Mahoney and Vic Thompson. Many other players and committee members also attended the service and the reception, which was held at popular Berkeley Café at the top of Park Street.

Bristol's Ladies' committee functioned for many years, providing teas for the players and organizing fund-raising activities. This picture, taken in the late 1940s, shows a group at a Ladies' committee dinner. From left to right, back row: George Gibbs, George Babbage, Tom Mahoney. Middle row: Pat Mahoney, Mary Golledge, Connie Griffin, Betty Crabbe, unknown. Front row: unknown, unknown, Mrs Bostock-Smith, Helen Burland, Maud Barrow, Mrs Quick.

Bristol travelled to France again, in February 1949, to play Cognac. This time, the outward journey was uneventful, but the return flight was diverted to Hurn airport because of fog at Whitchurch. As the team was not expected, there was some delay while the local customs officer was traced to the cinema and reluctantly hauled off to the airport. He was obviously anxious to return to the film, so he rushed through his inspection, much to the relief of the team as they were well stocked with brandy supplied by the president of the Cognac club! In terms of results, 1948/49 (George Gibbs's second year of captaincy) was Bristol's most successful season of the immediate post-war period. There were 27 victories – the most since 1934/35 – 3 draws and 13 defeats. The 1948/49 home programme, shown here, maintained the pre-war tradition of advertizing Georges' Beers on the front cover.

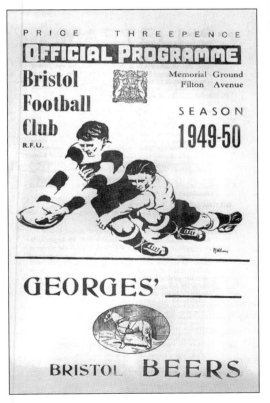

George Gibbs's final season of captaincy saw another good overall record, mainly thanks to an unbeaten run of 11 wins and 2 draws during the second half of the season. In all, 25 games were won. The regular home programme, shown here, now featured an illustration by Bristol's secretary, Percy Williams. This image proved an enduring one, and was used on the cover of the Colts Sevens programme, as recently as 1989.

D.G. Pratten first played for Bristol in 1945 as a three-quarter, but he made his name as a regular in the club's back row of the late 1940s and early '50s. A tremendously fit man, Doug Pratten captained Bristol and Gloucestershire and was still playing rugby for Old Cothamians in his late fifties. He taught at Cotham Grammar School for many years, and wrote a history of the school in 1991. In all, he played 217 games for Bristol, scoring 40 tries.

Doug Pratten, shown here running out on the occasion of his 200th appearance for club and county, was instrumental in bringing about a significant change in club policy in the early 1950s. When Jack Gregory was re-elected as captain in 1953, the players had unanimously proposed that Glyn Davies should have the post. At the annual general meeting, Doug Pratten proposed that, in future, the players should have a much greater say in the captaincy nominations. This was carried easily. Soon afterwards he left the club, relishing a new challenge at a slightly lower level with Cheltenham, but he continued to train at the Memorial Ground. In later life, Doug Pratten acted as Bristol's membership secretary and as secretary of the Old Players' Society. He died in 1997.

J.A. Gregory joined the club during the 1949/50 season, playing 129 games in all and scoring 73 tries. A winger, Jack Gregory was suspended for helping Huddersfield Rugby League Club, while stationed in the town just after the war. He was reinstated after a lengthy process, and gained his only England cap against Wales in 1949, as a Blackheath player. A noted sprinter, Jack Gregory appeared in two Olympic Games, winning a silver medal in the 4 x 100 metres relay in the London Games of 1948. He captained Bristol from 1952-1954.

Bristol's annual dinner was an integral feature of each season. This is the menu for the dinner on 1 May 1950, held at the Berkeley Café. The speakers included Bristol's pre-war rugby legend, Sam Tucker, and Adrian Stoop of Harlequins, a huge influence on the development of the game during the early years of the twentieth century.

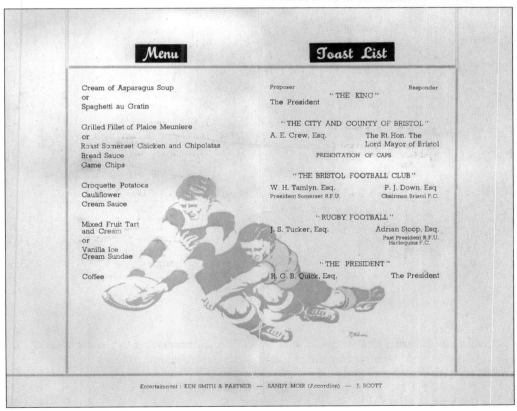

Menu

Cream of Asparagus Soup
or
Spaghetti au Gratin

Grilled Fillet of Plaice Meuniere
or
Roast Somerset Chicken and Chipolatas
Bread Sauce
Game Chips

Croquette Potatoes
Cauliflower
Cream Sauce

Mixed Fruit Tart
and Cream
or
Vanilla Ice
Cream Sundae

Coffee

Toast List

Proposer		Responder
	"THE KING"	
The President		
	"THE CITY AND COUNTY OF BRISTOL"	
A. E. Crew, Esq.		The Rt. Hon. The Lord Mayor of Bristol
	PRESENTATION OF CAPS	
	"THE BRISTOL FOOTBALL CLUB"	
W. H. Tamlyn. Esq.		P. J. Down. Esq
President Somerset R.F.U.		Chairman Bristol F.C.
	"RUGBY FOOTBALL"	
J. S. Tucker, Esq.		Adrian Stoop, Esq.
		Past President R.F.U. Harlequins F.C.
	"THE PRESIDENT"	
R. G. B. Quick, Esq.		The President

Entertainment : KEN SMITH & PARTNER — SANDY MOIR (Accordion) — J. SCOTT

A cheerful group of Bristol players enjoy a spot of pre-season training at the Memorial Ground. In the background is the covered terrace, popular with countless supporters until it was demolished in the late 1980s, in order to make way for the Centenary Stand. This picture dates from the late 1940s.

Still smiling, a slightly larger group poses for the cameraman. From left to right, back row: Bert Macdonald, Ken Griffin, Roy Clarke, Reg Redman, John Colston, Don Woodward, Tony Rees. Middle row: John Scott, John Webb, John Woodward, Peter Storkey, unknown, Eric McCall. Front row: Doug Pratten, Peter Jones, Gerry Murphy.

THERE WERE ONLY TWO WOODWARDS ON VIEW—WHICH WAS JUST AS WELL BECAUSE IF ANY MORE HAD TURNED UP —THE ANNEXE WOULD NEVER HAVE BEEN BIG ENOUGH—

John and Don Woodward, whose elder brother, Bill, had captained Bristol in 1936/37, were regular members of the Bristol pack around this time. John Woodward, a prop forward, played 95 first-team games from 1947-54. His younger brother, Don, was the club's regular hooker in the early 1950s, playing 172 games in all. He also played in an England trial in 1950. Both John, who died in 1994, and Don played county rugby for Gloucestershire. This caricature, presumably referring to pre-season training, pokes gentle fun at the brothers' respective weights.

In terms of results, the early 1950s saw a dip in the club's fortunes – Denzil Golledge's 1950/51 side just managed to stay in credit, winning 20 games, drawing 3, and losing 18. The first 4 games were lost and there was a further run of 5 defeats during October and November. Thereafter, an unbeaten run of 9 matches restored the team's confidence and, during this run, Bristol gained their first post-war victory over Cardiff. The 1950/51 team, from left to right, back row: P.J. Williams (secretary), J.R.E. Bryan (treasurer), R.G.B. Quick, A.J. Owens Britton. Third row: A.M. Bain, E.G. Hopton, R.W. Muller, A.E. Macdonald, M.D. Corbett, R.N. Clarke. Second row: J.A. Scott, K.C. Smith, D.W. Woodward, R.S. Lloyd, D. Gunson, J. Holt. Front row: E.E. McCall, P.L.E. Storkey, D.G. Golledge (captain), P.J. Down (chairman), D.G. Pratten, G. Lovell, J.A. Gregory.

Bristol's captain for 1950/51 was centre three-quarter D.G. Golledge. A product of Bristol Grammar School, Denzil Golledge played in many positions behind the scrum for Bristol, and also appeared in the pack. He had one season with Cleve before joining the RAF, becoming a Bristol player after his demobilization. Denzil Golledge, who died in 1980, also played cricket for Frenchay and was the son-in-law of Bristol Chairman Percy Down.

Winger K.C. Smith played 172 games for Bristol between 1950 and 1959, scoring 68 tries. Keith Smith's runs up the left wing were often completed with a characteristic flying leap over the try line. He played county rugby for Somerset.

Another Bristol regular at this time was M.D. Corbett, son of the great Len Corbett, Bristol's famous centre three-quarter of the 1920s. A centre himself, Michael Corbett never captained his club, but he did have the honour of leading the Western Counties against the touring South Africans at Bristol in 1952. During the 1951/52 season, Corbett captained Somerset, while his club colleague, Doug Pratten, captained Gloucestershire. Michael Corbett later played for Clifton.

An intriguing mixture of youth and experience lines up for Bristol United, before the game with Richmond 'A' on 17 February 1951. Standing on the extreme left is George Gibbs, by now based in Newcastle, and making a one-off reappearance, while amongst the younger element is Arthur Sheppard, who was at the beginning of a Bristol career which was to span the ensuing decade. Arthur Sheppard is second from right in the front row, next to captain for the day, Ken Griffin. Bristol United won this game 17-3.

Despite having a top quality captain in Doug Pratten, the 1951/52 side produced the poorest record for many years, winning only 15 games. The team did not play as badly as the final record suggests, but many games were lost through weak play at the end of the matches. The highlight of the season was a double against Harlequins. From left to right, back row: P.J. Williams (secretary), J.R.E. Bryan (treasurer), D. Gunson, J.A. Scott, J.E. Woodward, R.H. Muller, M.J. Howell, A.M. Bain, P.L.E. Storkey, R.T. Moule, P.J. Down (chairman). Middle row: K.C. Smith, K.R. Griffin, D. Day, D.G. Pratten (captain), J. Tucker (president), J.A. Gregory, J. Holt, B.W. Rowsell, M.D. Corbett. Front row: R. Standing, W.P. Donnelly.

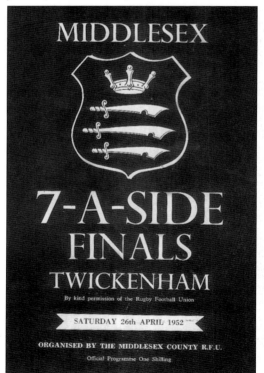

At the end of the season, Bristol were invited to be one of the guest sides in the prestigious Middlesex Sevens tournament at Twickenham. Unfortunately, Jack Gregory was training for the Helsinki Olympics and could not play. Without him, Bristol managed to defeat Old Millhillians 11-8, but lost 16-5 to eventual the champions, Wasps. This picture shows the programme for the tournament.

The 1952/53 season, the first of Jack Gregory's two terms as skipper, saw an improvement in the club's fortunes. 23 games were won, and the arrival of fly-half Glyn Davies was a major boost. His trademark cross-kicks provided Gregory with many of the 19 tries he scored during the season. The team hit its best form at the season's end, losing only one of its last 12 games, and that by just a point against Cardiff. From left to right, back row: T.A.B. Mahoney, A.R. Northover (treasurer), J.E. Woodward, D.W. Woodward, J.A. Scott, M.J. Howell, K.C. Smith, A.R. Sheppard, R.T. Moule, P.J. Williams (secretary), P.J. Down (chairman). Front row: G.F. Cripps, A.M. Bain, T.U. Wells, J.A. Gregory (captain), J. Tucker (president), P.L.E. Storkey, D.G. Pratten, G. Davies, G. Lovell.

The former captain passes to his successor – Doug Pratten hands on to Jack Gregory, during Bristol's opening game of 1952/53. The opposition, Lydney, ran Bristol close, before going down 12-11.

Outside half Glyn Davies joined Bristol in 1952, having previously gained 11 Welsh caps. A Cambridge Blue, who also played for Pontypridd, he appeared in 2 Victory Internationals while still at school. He played 47 games for Bristol, before returning to Wales. The brother-in-law of opera singer Sir Geraint Evans, Glyn Davies died in 1976.

Bristol's record in 1953/54 was not quite as good as that of the previous season, with only 19 games won. However, on 20 March 1954, Bristol fielded two first XVs on the same day, defeating London Welsh at the Memorial Ground and United Services at Portsmouth. In April, the team went on a short tour of the north-west of England, defeating Waterloo but losing to Birkenhead Park. This picture shows the tour party in front of their coach.

Bristol became a part of rugby history on 1 May 1954, when they were invited to play in the first Welsh seven-a-side tournament. This event became known as the Snelling Sevens, and was a popular end-of-season occasion for many years, before dwindling appeal brought about its demise in 1995. Unfortunately, Bristol did not progress past the opening round, losing 6-3 to Aberavon. This is the tournament programme.

RUGBY   FOOTBALL

FIRST WELSH SEVEN-A-SIDE TOURNAMENT

Guest Side : BRISTOL

NEWPORT ATHLETIC CLUB

SATURDAY, MAY 1st, 1954

COMMENCING   -   2 p.m.

Official Programme   -   6D.

BRISTOL

The Bristol United XV of 1953/54 played 29 games, winning 16, drawing 1, and losing 12. Skipper Dennis Skinner played in all but three of the matches, and one of the highlights was an enormous 72-6 victory over Berry Hill. From left to right, back row: D. Hull, L. Wagland, G.W. Allen, G.M. Dummett, P. Symes. Middle row: H. Nicholas, A.R. Northover (treasurer), R.W. Trott, T.E. Base, R. Challis, D. Edgecombe, I. Macdonald, B.R.J. Beesley, B.G. Richards, S. Harvey, R.B. Stuart, D. Wyatt, R.G.B. Quick, P.J. Williams (secretary). Front row: B.J. Broad, D.W. Neate, D.J. Skinner (captain), P.J. Down (chairman), M. MacCarthy, W. White, J.F. Duggan.

B.J. Broad played his first game for
Bristol in 1951, and made a total of
157 appearances, mainly as a
winger. John Broad joined the club
after serving in the Royal Artillery,
and he scored 61 tries for the first
team. He was vice-captain during
his final season, and also played for
Gloucestershire. Later, he became a
founder member of Thornbury
RFC, playing his final game of
rugby at the age of sixty. John
Broad died in 2001.

A.R. Sheppard, an England Schools' cap, made
his Bristol debut in 1950, at the age of seventeen,
and went on to play 107 first-team games in a
career often blighted by injury. Joining the club
from Old Redcliffians, Arthur Sheppard was originally a flank forward, but later converted to the
second row with great success. His trademark
broad grin is a regular feature of team
photographs throughout the 1950s.

Two
The Blake Era
1954-1961

Bert Macdonald's 1954/55 team won 25 games and, in scoring 475 points, recorded the highest points total since 1928/29. Bristol were hammered 38-3 at Cardiff in January, but recovered to enjoy a successful second half of the season, during which only 5 games were lost and Northampton were defeated twice. New Zealander T.U. Wells, a full-back, was Bristol vice-captain during both of Macdonald's seasons of captaincy. Tom Wells, who died in 2001, played 105 games for Bristol between 1952 and 1956, and also represented Gloucestershire. From left to right, back row: A.R. Northover (treasurer), D.W. Woodward, J. Trott, A.E. Carter, G.F. Cripps, T.A.B. Mahoney, R.C. Hawkes, D.W. Neate, A.R. Sheppard, P.J. Williams (secretary). Middle row: R.W. Trott, B.J. Broad, R. Challis, A.E. Macdonald (captain), R.G.B. Quick (chairman), T.U. Wells, B.G. Richards, G.R. Thomas, G. Troote. Front row: M.G. Ellery, T.E. Base, J.N. Blake, E.R. Blackman, G.W. Davis.

A.E. Macdonald played his first game for Bristol in 1948, and went on to beat Fred Coventry's longstanding First XV appearance record, playing a total of 344 matches. One of Bristol's greatest ever forwards, Bert Macdonald captained the club for two seasons from 1954, and also played for Gloucestershire. He was selected for a Scottish trial and was considered unlucky not to be awarded a Scottish cap. Bert Macdonald, whose brother Ian also played for the club, captained Bristol United at the end of his distinguished career, finally retiring in 1961. When he moved to London, he helped to form the London-Bristol Society and thus kept in touch with his former team-mates, whenever Bristol played in the capital.

The Cardiff debacle proved a watershed for the club. Bristol's heaviest defeat for forty-two years was the catalyst for a change of policy. With the backing of the selection committee, Macdonald introduced a new approach to training and tactics. Bristol adopted a more open style of play, which was to culminate in the glorious seasons of the late 1950s under John Blake's leadership. The illustration shows the programme for the Cardiff game, for which, incidentally, the home team was not at full strength.

1955/56, Bert Macdonald's second season of captaincy, heralded the start of a golden period for the club. Bristol's increased fitness, and willingness to run the ball, led to 31 victories, equalling the club record. From left to right, back row: P. Smith, G. Troote, T.E. Base, M.G. Ellery. Third row: P.J. Williams (secretary), A.R. Northover (treasurer), G.F. Cripps, R.C. Hawkes, F.J. Williams, D.W. Neate, J. Trott, R. Challis, T.A.B. Mahoney, R.R. Morris. Second row, seated: E.R. Blackman, J.A. Scott, G.W. Davis, T.U. Wells, R.G.B. Quick (chairman), A.E. Macdonald (captain), D.W. Griffiths, G.R. Thomas, J.D. Thorne. Front row: B.J. Broad, R.A. Dash.

During 1955/56, only one defeat was suffered at home, when St Mary's Hospital beat Bristol 8-6 in October. Gloucester, Leicester and Bath were all beaten twice, and there were victories over Newport and Llanelly. Most satisfying of all, however, was a win against Cardiff, which provided ample revenge for the previous season's humiliation. The season ended with 10 consecutive victories. Bristol's penultimate game was at Weston-Super-Mare, and resulted in a hard-fought 6-0 victory. This photograph shows second-row forward, Derek Neate, scoring Bristol's first try after fifteen minutes of play. A second-half try from Bert Macdonald was the only other score.

BRISTOL FOOTBALL CLUB

R.F.U.

OFFICIAL
PROGRAMME
PRICE
3D.

SEASON
1955-1956
Memorial Ground
Filton Avenue

THE COMMITTEE AND PLAYERS WISH YOU A HAPPY CHRISTMAS
Cardiff have always been very welcome visitors to Bristol, and although their record this season is not to be compared with their scintillating achievements of recent years, Bristol will be fully tested this afternoon. Our visitor's lack of success in September and October was due in part to the absence of G. M. Griffiths, C. I. Morgan and H. Morris—members of the British Lions party. The retirement of B. L. Williams and the injury to W. R. Willis, were also contributory factors—the Welsh scrum-half had the misfortune to break an ankle.

Bristol spent a most unhappy afternoon at Arms Park last January and we suffered our heaviest defeat for years. In the return match in February, however, we had much the better of the exchanges yet lost because we wasted our scoring chances.

The collection to-day is for the Bristol Junior Rugby Combination, that very important organisation in local Rugger and we are confident our spectators will show their goodwill towards the juniors by contributing generously.

It is regretted that a severe cut in our application for Stand tickets for the England v. Wales match will necessitate a ballot. All applications for Stand tickets will enter the ballot, including those who consented to a lower grade ticket if no Stand available. The latter, if unsuccessful in the ballot will be guaranteed either an Enclosure or Field ticket according to our allocation. It is hoped to distribute tickets in the first week of January. All applications for England v. Ireland will be met.

After to-day's match, tickets for the England v. Wales Schools' International on the Memorial Ground on 7th April, 1956, will be on sale at the programme hut (at the top of the Enclosure slope)—Enclosure 2/6; Ground 2/-. Application forms for Stand tickets will also be issued.

On Boxing Day the Schools' Senior Cup Final will be played on this ground, kick-off 11 a.m. and the following is the list of our other holiday and New Year attractions:—

		kick-off
Boxing Day—Newbridge	...	2.45 p.m.
Tuesday, 27th December—Old Merchant Taylors	...	2.45 p.m.
Saturday, 31st December—Llanelly	...	2.45 p.m.
Saturday, 7th January—Harlequins	...	2.45 p.m.

BRISTOL & DISTRICT RUGBY SUPPORTERS' CLUB

JOIN THE
SUPPORTERS' CLUB
MEMBERSHIP FEE 1-

Hon. Secretary   C. A. C. ELLICOTT
1, BURGHLEY ROAD
BRISTOL.

Telephone Bristol 44994

Bristol's programmes were reduced to four pages during the 1950s. This is the programme for the highly prized victory over Cardiff on Christmas Eve 1955. The visitors' star outside-half, Cliff Morgan, was away on his honeymoon, but Cardiff still fielded five internationals. A last-minute penalty from Gordon Cripps won this thrilling match for Bristol. The final score was 11-8.

P.L.E. Storkey, a speedy front-row forward, played 147 matches for Bristol from 1946 to 1956, and subsequently served on Bristol's committee for many years. Peter Storkey, who died in 1976, captained the Bristol United team of 1955/56, which played 29 games, winning 26, drawing once and losing twice. The photograph shows Peter Storkey (holding ball) with this outstanding side.

Bristol had long felt the need for a proper clubhouse. A makeshift social club had operated in part of the club's gymnasium, but, in 1956, plans were prepared for something more permanent. A special game was arranged, against a team led by Cardiff and Wales scrum-half Rex Willis, to raise funds for the new building. The match, which was not counted in official records, was won 23-17 by the visitors, and led to a series of such encounters. This is the programme from the game. The clubhouse itself was finally opened on 11 October 1958.

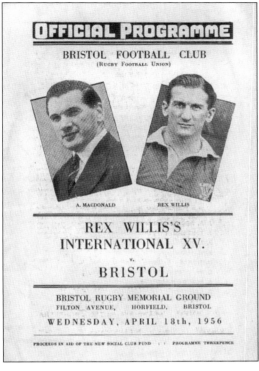

R.C. Hawkes, a second-row forward with previous first class experience at Northampton, joined Bristol in 1954, playing 92 matches for the club. While at Northampton, he played for the Barbarians and was a member of the East Midlands XV which won the County Championship in 1951. He was also an England trialist. Bristol were delighted to welcome a player of his experience, and he was appointed captain for the 1956/57 season.

Scrum-half Gordon Lovell played 140 games for the club from 1950 to 1958. He learned his rugby at local club Cleve and he also played for Sheffield, Maesteg, Newport and Abertillery, as well as representing Western Clubs against South African Universities in 1957. A long-serving Bristol committee-man, he is currently the secretary of Bristol Rugby Former Players. He is shown here receiving the ball from his captain, Dick Hawkes, during Bristol's 1956/57 victory over Cardiff.

Dick Hawkes' 1956/57 team created two new records. The record number of wins in a season was extended to 33, and the side scored 573 points, beating the 556 registered by the 1928/29 team. From left to right, back row: W.F. Bartlett, A.R. Northover (treasurer), T.A.B. Mahoney, P. Smith, A.R. Sheppard, D.W. Neate, K.C. Smith, D. Wyatt, J. Bull, D.A. Brinton, H. Nicholas, P.L.E. Storkey, J. Purnell. Third row: J. Woodward, R.R. Morris, R.V. Muller, C.R. Setter, R.A. Lyons, C.M. Hollister, K. Palmer, F.J. Williams, G.F. Cripps, A.E. Macdonald, R. Challis, J. Trott, B. Long, J.M. Hellings, J.N. Hazell, F.J. Coventry, P.W. Redwood. Second row: E. Pidgeon, C.A.C. Ellicott, R.V. Bridgeman, J.D. Thorne, G.R. Thomas, B.J. Broad, R.G.B. Quick (chairman), R.C. Hawkes (captain), D.W. Griffiths, R.A. Dash, G. Troote, J.R.E. Bryan, P.J. Williams (secretary). Front row: G. Lovell, R. Phibbin, T.W. Jones, A.D. Allen, D.R. Earl, J.N. Blake, M.G. Ellery, T.E. Base.

Once again, open rugby was the key to Bristol's success. Only 4 away games were lost, and Bristol won at both Newport and Llanelly. Bath and Leicester were defeated twice, Cardiff were beaten at the Memorial Ground and, for the first time since the fixture started in 1894, Bristol beat Swansea twice in a season. Perhaps the most remarkable victory of the season was the one at Newport. Bristol travelled to Rodney Parade minus three key players, who were all involved in an England trial at the Memorial Ground. Newport, who were at full strength, led 8-0 at half time, but Bristol staged an astonishing recovery after the break, eventually winning 19-8. This picture shows the match programme.

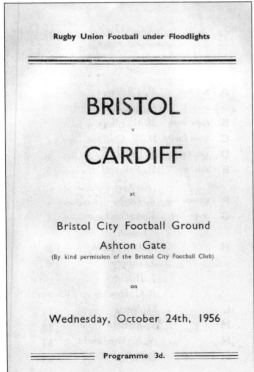

It was during this season that Bristol began staging occasional games under floodlights at Bristol City FC's Ashton Gate ground. Floodlit rugby was something of a novelty at the time, and the games, which tended to be fast and open, did not count in the club's official records. This is the programme for the first of these matches, which visitors Cardiff won 20-13, in front of a crowd of over 11,000.

Later in the season, Harlequins came to Ashton Gate, defeating Bristol 12-11. Before the kick-off, the teams were photographed together.

M.G. Ellery, a winger, was a key member of the successful Bristol teams led by Macdonald, Hawkes and, particularly, John Blake. Blake gave him carte blanche to roam around the field and, as a result, he scored as many tries on the left as the right. Mike Ellery scored 251 tries in 347 matches for Bristol, a record only surpassed in later years by Alan Morley. But even the prolific Morley couldn't top the record of 44 tries scored in a season by Ellery in 1961/62. A county-level sprinter who used athletics to enhance his rugby skills, Ellery suffered by playing at a time when unimaginative national selectors were sceptical about Bristol's open approach to the game. He had a trial for England and represented the local selections against the major touring sides, but he was never chosen for an international.

Another novelty during 1956/57 was the visit of a team from Bucharest. The Romanians played Bristol on 19 September, drawing 6-6. The game was yet another 'unofficial' fixture. The pennant illustrated was presented to Bristol captain Dick Hawkes before the kick-off.

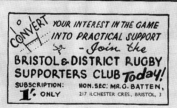

BRISTOL FOOTBALL CLUB

OFFICIAL PROGRAMME
PRICE 3D.

R.F.U.

SEASON 1956-1957
Memorial Ground
Filton Avenue

This is the first time we have had the privilege of being hosts to a team from Rumania, and we give a very special welcome to these Rugby footballers from the Continent. This team from Bucarest is selected from five teams and their strength is shewn by their play today.

We trust their visit to the West Country will be a pleasant memory to them, and when they return home, they will carry the best wishes for the future from all Rugby footballers in the City of Bristol.

CONVERT YOUR INTEREST IN THE GAME INTO PRACTICAL SUPPORT — Join the BRISTOL & DISTRICT RUGBY SUPPORTERS CLUB Today!

SUBSCRIPTION: 1/- ONLY
HON. SEC: MR. G. BATTEN, 217 ILCHESTER CRES., BRISTOL, 3

The match itself was fast and exciting. The visitors led 6-0 at half time and Bristol only managed to draw level in the final fifteen minutes to finish at 6-6. This is the programme from the game.

43

Originally a scrum-half and, occasionally, a centre, the versatile T.E. Base eventually settled in the back row of the Bristol scrum. Terry Base enjoyed a long and successful career, playing 295 games between 1953 and 1967, and scoring 75 tries. He went to Cotham Grammar School and played for Old Cothamians before joining Bristol. He captained the National Federation of Boys' Clubs against Wales in 1951, and played regularly for Gloucestershire, including the 1959 county final *v.* Warwickshire. In 1962, he left Bristol to study in America, and subsequently returned to lecture at Southampton University. Terry Base died in 2000.

Bob Challis, a full-back, gained 3 England caps in 1957, a year which provided England with its last Grand Slam until 1980. He created great interest on his international debut, by electing to place kick penalties into touch instead of kicking out of hand. Educated at Bristol Cathedral School, he played for Old Cathedralians and made 103 appearances for Bristol. He played county rugby for Somerset, and also played cricket for Somerset Second XI. Bob Challis died in 2000.

D.W. Griffiths played 134 games for Bristol between 1951 and 1961, scoring 38 tries. He attended Marksbury Road Secondary School and gained an England Schools' cap against Wales in 1949. Chiefly a centre, Derek Griffiths joined Bristol from local club, Cotham Park, played county rugby for Somerset, and, whilst on National Service, also played for Dorset and Wiltshire.

Bristol United, under captain G.R. Thomas, played 32 games in 1956/57, winning 22, drawing 3, and losing 7. Graham Thomas, who captained the side in the following season as well, was a firm believer in running rugby and encouraged throwing the ball around and starting attacks from all parts of the field. As a result of this, younger players were introduced to the club's running style. Graham Thomas is shown here (holding ball) with his successful United squad.

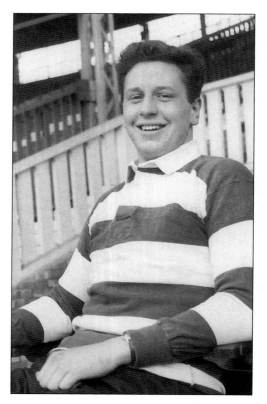

D.W. Neate was introduced to rugby by Les Williams, the Welsh international, at Portway School. A second row or number eight forward, Derek Neate was invited to join Bristol after being spotted playing for Avonmouth, and he made his first team debut in 1953. In an exceptionally long career, he made 393 appearances. His last First XV match was in 1972, and he played for Bristol United as late as 1976. One of Bristol's finest ever forwards, he played 48 times for Gloucestershire, including the 1959 county final, and represented the RAF in the 1958 Inter-Services tournament. He appeared in 3 England trials and was very close to a full cap, being reserve to travel on several occasions. Derek Neate captained Bristol for two separate periods, from 1961-63 and from 1965-67. His 73 tries are indicative of his personal fitness and his valuable contribution to Bristol's fifteen-man style of rugby.

J.N. Blake made his First XV debut for Bristol in 1953, and played 339 games in all, scoring 92 tries and a club-record 32 drop goals. John Blake, who could play in the centre but was usually to be found at outside half, was a truly gifted leader and a genuine inspiration to those around him. No individual has exercised so much influence during the history of the club, and his four seasons of captaincy are affectionately known as 'The Blake Era'. His philosophy was to run and pass at all opportunities. Kicking out of hand was discouraged, and attacking moves were regularly started from behind Bristol's own line. Training consisted simply of running, passing and perfecting a handful of set moves.

John Blake instilled a tremendous team spirit. His team-mates had enormous respect for him and he took full responsibility for Bristol's style of play. If he set his mind on something, he would achieve it, and his amazing memory for the smallest details of previous games was a great asset. His style of leadership was that of gentle persuasion. John Blake later became headmaster of St Joseph's School, Crawley, but died at the tragically early age of forty-nine in 1983, and was much mourned by those who knew him and who had had the privilege of playing rugby with him.

1957/58, the first season of John Blake's captaincy, saw records being broken again. 34 games were won and 779 points scored. From left to right, back row: F.J. Williams, R. Challis, M.G. Ellery, P.J. Colston, B. Long, J.A. Radford, P. Smith, K. Palmer, T.A.B. Mahoney, D. Wyatt, D.E.J. Watt, A.R. Sheppard, D.W. Neate, B.P.D. Dawson, J.M. Hellings, R.C. Hawkes. Middle row: R.R. Morris, V.E. Ball, P.W. Redwood, J. Purnell, H. Nicholas, W. Sullivan, E.R. Blackman, C.M. Hollister, T.E. Base, R.V. Bridgeman, K.C. Smith, G.F. Cripps, C. Kimmins, J. Bull, M. Davey, P. Williams, J.D. Thorne, C.R Setter, J.N. Hazell, P.L.E. Storkey. Front row: J.R.E. Bryan, C.A.C. Ellicott, R.A. Dash, D.W. Griffiths, T.W. Jones, A.E. Macdonald, R.G.B. Quick (chairman), J.N. Blake (captain), G.R. Thomas, J. Trott, G.W. Davis, G. Lovell, F.J. Coventry, A.R. Northover (treasurer), P.J. Williams (secretary).

One of Bristol's rare defeats during this season was on their visit to Twickenham to play Harlequins. Their hosts won a high-scoring game, 33-18. The picture shows J.M. Hellings, of Bristol, sending out a pass. John Hellings, a flanker who later converted to prop forward, played 78 games for the club between 1953 and 1962, before returning to captain his original team, Cotham Park. He played 3 games for Gloucestershire.

Bath and Northampton were defeated twice during 1957/58, and Bristol won at Swansea again. On two occasions, there were home and away first-team fixtures on the same day. All 4 games were won, on the second occasion by the identical scoreline of 32-3. In November 1957, Bristol paid their first visit to France since 1949, defeating CA Beglais (33-6) and Arcachon (38-8). This picture shows John Blake shaking hands with the Beglais captain, Baudorre.

Bristol's visit to Birkenhead Park in April 1958 was looked on as something of an unofficial championship decider. Park had been dubbed 'Cock of the North' by the local media, and Bristol were definitely the strongest team in the south. In the event, Bristol won easily (28-9) despite being reduced to thirteen players through injuries. This was long before replacements were permitted for injured players. This is the programme from the match.

At the end of the 1957/58 season, Bristol won 8 consecutive games. The first 15 matches of the following season ended in victory. This club record of 23 consecutive wins was finally brought to an end by Wasps in November (6-5), but the team went on to enjoy another season of success under John Blake. There were 34 wins again, and the point-scoring record was increased to 792. Bristol's style of rugby, now universally known as 'Bristol Fashion', was a great crowd-puller and attendances rose at away grounds when Bristol played there. From left to right, back row: A.R. Northover (treasurer), D.J. Weeks, J. New, A.E. Macdonald, D.E.J. Watt, D.W. Neate, L.D. Watts, J.D. Thorne, P.J. Williams (secretary). Middle row: R.R. Morris, M.R. Walters, R.V. Bridgeman, R. Challis, J.A. Radford, D. St G. Hazell, M.G. Ellery, J.R.E. Bryan, T.A.B. Mahoney. Front row: R.A. Dash, C. Kimmins, T.E. Base, C.M. Hollister, J.N. Blake (captain), C.R. Setter (president), G.F. Cripps, B.W. Redwood, D.W. Griffiths, T.W. Jones, G.W. Davis.

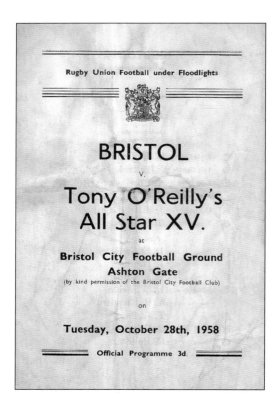

Rugby Union Football under Floodlights

BRISTOL

v.

Tony O'Reilly's All Star XV.

at

Bristol City Football Ground Ashton Gate

(by kind permission of the Bristol City Football Club)

on

Tuesday, October 28th, 1958

Official Programme 3d.

Floodlit rugby at Ashton Gate continued with the visit of Tony O'Reilly's XV in October 1958. O'Reilly, the charismatic Irish winger and star of two 1950s Lions' tours, was friendly with Bristol committee-man Jim Bryan, and had also brought a XV to play Bristol the previous season. Floodlit rugby provided Bristol with the perfect stage to reach a wider audience, and this thrilling encounter ended with winger T. Wynne Jones scoring a last-minute try, which Gordon Cripps converted for a 26-25 victory.

Bristol made their first visit to Ireland to play a Sunday celebration match, as part of a Dublin rugby weekend, which had featured an Irish victory over England the previous day. It was not the best of days for the Bristol side. They had defeated a tough St Luke's College side the day before, in a very abrasive match from which they were still feeling the after-effects, and when Laurie Watts damaged his shin early on, Bristol effectively took on the Irish side a man short. The game was Bristol's way of saying thank you to Tony O'Reilly for bringing teams over to play the club. In what was a disappointing game, Old Belvedere won 21-3. This is the programme from the game.

Old Belvedere R.F.C.

OLD BELVEDERE

RUGBY FOOTBALL CLUB

v

BRISTOL

FOOTBALL CLUB

ANGLESEA ROAD

SUNDAY, 15th FEBRUARY, 1959

Kick-off 3.15 p.m.

F. X. KELLY, LTD.

Tailors and Outfitters

48 GRAFTON STREET, DUBLIN

Suppliers of O.B.R.F.C. Blazers, Scarves and Ties

Programme - 3d.

Winger R.V. Bridgeman played 85 games for Bristol between 1957 and 1964, and would have played far more, but for a series of unfortunate injuries. A Somerset sprinting champion, Ron Bridgeman, who also played soccer for Weston-Super-Mare, joined Bristol from Dings Crusaders. His impressive speed bought him 60 tries, and a further 124 in 108 games for Bristol United. He played regularly for Somerset, and was Bristol's physiotherapist for nine seasons, after a dreadful knee injury had finished his playing career.

Matches at Gloucester were usually torrid affairs, frequently with close scores and the home side generally winning. In February 1959, Bristol headed up the A38 once more to the lion's den of Kingsholm. They recorded a resounding victory 19-6, scoring five tries and playing with the wonderful flare typical of the Blake era. The Bristol centres, John Radford and Laurie Watts, tore holes in the Gloucester defence and set up tries for Mike Ellery, Fred Williams, Ron Bridgeman (two) and Watts himself. Here, Bridgeman crashes over for his second try, despite the attentions of Gloucester's Brian Green.

Goal-kicking number eight forward Gordon Cripps played his first game for Bristol in November 1951. By the time he retired at the end of the 1961/62 season, he had scored an amazing 1,310 points in 291 matches. His 152 in 1954/55 broke the club record, which he went on to better again over the following seasons, reaching his zenith in 1958/59 with 230 points. This record stood until 1972, when it was beaten by Alan Pearn. Gordon Cripps learnt to play rugby at St George School, and also played for the Imperial Club. He played in an England trial in 1954 and captained Gloucestershire in the 1959 county final. When he retired, the following appeared in Bristol's annual report: 'Those of us who had the great pleasure of watching his amazingly accurate kicking will realize that we had been watching a master.'

In March 1959, Bristol entered the Oxford Sevens, losing 23-13 to Wasps in the final. The Bristol team pictured here are, from left to right, back row: Dave Watt, John Blake, Laurie Watts, Pat Mills. Front row: Derek Neate, Bill Redwood, John Thorne. A month later, Bristol were at Twickenham again, as guests in the Middlesex Sevens. Unfortunately, the team put in a disappointing performance, losing 8-5 to London Irish in the opening round.

John Blake's 1959/60 team has claims to be considered one of the greatest in the club's history. By maintaining an entertaining, open style of play, this side broke the scoring record yet again with 834 points – and this at a time when a try was only worth three points. 36 games were won – another new record – and when Blake dropped three goals in an exciting Easter Monday win against Northampton, he became the first (and, to date, the only) Bristol player to achieve this feat. Bristol visited France again, defeating Clermont-Ferrand (25-18) and there were doubles over Bath, Gloucester and Leicester. Strangely, amidst all this success, no Bristol player was selected for England, and it was felt that the unadventurous national selectors were wary of the team's modern methods. Equally strangely, attendances dropped at the Memorial Ground! This is the programme from Bristol's 25-11 victory at Kingsholm in September 1959.

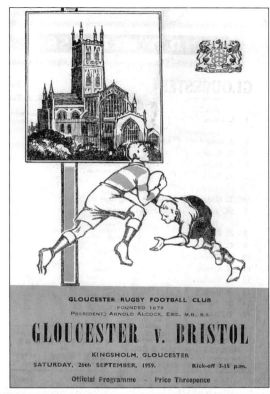

GLOUCESTER RUGBY FOOTBALL CLUB
FOUNDED 1873
PRESIDENT: Arnold Alcock, Esq., M.B., B.S.

GLOUCESTER v. BRISTOL

KINGSHOLM, GLOUCESTER
SATURDAY, 26th SEPTEMBER, 1959.   Kick-off 3-15 p.m.

Official Programme - Price Threepence

Here is John Blake's great 1959/60 side. From left to right, back row: J. New, R.V. Bridgeman, T.A.B. Mahoney, A.R. Sheppard, D.W. Neate. Middle row: R.R. Morris, R.G.B. Quick (chairman), J.M. Hellings, D.J. Weeks, T.E. Base, D.E.J. Watt, L.D. Watts, C.M. Hollister, J.A. Radford, J.D. Thorne, A.R. Northover (treasurer), P.J. Williams (secretary). Front row: P.J. Colston, C.T. Allen, L. Davies, J.N. Blake (captain), C.R. Setter (president), A.E. Macdonald, M.G. Ellery, B.W. Redwood, R.A. Dash.

Another star of the Blake era, centre D.J. Weeks played 213 first-team games. He scored exactly 50 tries for Bristol, and scored his 50th in his 200th game. David Weeks, who was vice-captain in 1961/62, learnt his rugby at Bristol Grammar School and later played for Old Bristolians. During his time as a student, he captained the Bristol University First XV and later represented Gloucestershire, as well as Western Counties, when they played the South Africans at Gloucester in 1960.

J.A. Radford, shown here during pre-season training, was another regular centre during the Blake era and beyond. Like David Weeks, John Radford was versatile enough to be used on the wing on occasion. He played 166 games in all, scoring 56 tries, and appeared for Gloucestershire in the 1959 county final. Later that year, he appeared in an England trial. John Radford, whose son, Jim, played once for the club in 1995, made his final appearance against Blackheath in 1970 and fittingly converted Bristol's last try – the only goal kick of his Bristol career.

L.D. Watts, another of Gloucestershire's county finalists in 1959, played 124 Bristol games, usually as a centre. An accomplished goal kicker, Laurie Watts was a fine all-round sportsman. He attended Bristol Grammar School and went on to Oxford University, where he won rugby blues in 1957 and 1958 and played regular cricket, although not in the Varsity match. He was an England trialist in 1958/59, and came close to a cap when selected as a travelling reserve. Laurie Watts often played cricket for Gloucestershire Second XI and once represented the First XI, scoring 0 and 46 against Surrey at Bristol in 1958. Laurie Watts' father, a builder, named Lawrence Grove in Dursley after his young son. Laurie Watts died in 1997.

1960/61, John Blake's fourth and final season of captaincy, was, statistically, something of a disappointment. Despite having basically the same squad of players, Bristol victories dropped to 31, and 13 games were lost. There was, however, one excuse – the weather! This was a particularly wet season, and the Memorial Ground became so badly affected that Bristol's open style was hard to maintain. Cardiff's attempt to play Bristol under the floodlights at Cardiff City's Ninian Park was twice thwarted by the weather. When the game was eventually played, Bristol emerged as winners, 19-14. The picture shows the official programme.

Bristol's match against Devonport Services on 22 April 1961 marked John Blake's final home game as captain. He had also captained Somerset during the season, having previously played for, and captained, Gloucestershire. This picture, besides marking an historic moment, perfectly indicates the type of weather which Bristol had to suffer during the season. A barely recognizable Blake is carried and applauded by his mud-caked team-mates and the touch judge, Tom Mahoney, at the conclusion of a 25-3 victory, on what appears to be a swamp.

Back-row forward, Len Davies, formed a speedy breakaway unit with Terry Base and Gordon Cripps, which was well suited to the club's handling style. Davies, who was born in Treorchy and studied at St Luke's College, Exeter, made 171 first-team appearances, scoring 41 tries. He was a regular Somerset player.

Reg Quick, a Bristol player from 1913-28 and a committee-man for many years, resigned from the committee at the end of 1960/61 following a spell as chairman. His lifelong devotion to the club was marked by a special presentation. This picture shows Bristol's president, Cecil Setter, giving a silver salver to Reg Quick (left), watched by their wives. Bristol's annual report of that season states: 'We who have worked with him for so many years realize what a loss he will be to Rugby Football.'

Bristol enjoyed a friendly relationship with Bristol Rovers Football Club for many years. When both clubs had fixtures in London on the same day, the teams regularly travelled by train together. The Rovers players were fascinated by the social life enjoyed by their amateur friends. Bristol even put on social evenings for the Rovers players, at times when such excesses wouldn't affect on-field performance. This is the programme for a game of 'Socby' between the clubs. Socby was a twelve-a-side soccer match played with a rugby ball. This game in 1961 attracted over 7,000 spectators to Rovers' Eastville Stadium, for what was an hilarious fund-raising event.

Bristol Rovers Football Club, Limited

(FOUNDED 1883)

President:—HIS GRACE THE DUKE OF BEAUFORT, K.G., P.C., G.C.V.O.
Directors:—H. J. Hampden Alpass (*Chairman*), J. P. Hare, P. W. Hon, Dr. M. A. Nicholson,
D. Simpson, Con. A. L. Stevens, G. W. Vaughan.
Manager:—B. J. Tann. *Secretary:*—R. A. Meules.
Medical Officer:—Dr. W. T. Cussen, M.B., Ch.B., E.A.O.
Trainers:—G. A. Williams, W. McArthur *Coaches:*—J. H. Pitt; J. B. Doyle.

Regd. Office and Ground :—

EASTVILLE (BRISTOL) STADIUM

TUESDAY, MAY 2nd, 1961. KICK-OFF 7.30 P.M.

BRISTOL ROVERS
v.
BRISTOL (Rugby) F.C.

"SOCBY"

. . . . . played under Association Football Rules with a Rugby ball, twelve-a-side.

The main purpose of the game is to raise funds for Charity, but it will provide players, officials and spectators with an opportunity for relaxation, and we hope, worthwhile entertainment and good fun.

On behalf of those who will benefit, we thank you for your support.

OFFICIAL PROGRAMME — 2d.

R.A. Dash played much of his early Bristol rugby at outside half, but was later used at full-back when John Blake claimed the fly-half berth. Roy Dash played 160 games from 1955-62, scoring 104 points, and also represented Gloucestershire. While teaching at Henbury School, he helped to found local club, Aretians. Roy Dash died in 1993.

Goal-kicking prop forward D. St G. Hazell, who captained Taunton School in 1949, was capped 4 times for England as a Leicester player in 1955. David Hazell joined Bristol the following year, and made 241 appearances, scoring 483 points. He took over from Gordon Cripps as the club's chief goal kicker, and played until 1964. David Hazell, who had previously played county rugby for Leicestershire, was made captain of Somerset in the 1963/64 season, during which time he was also Bristol's vice-captain.

Three
From Neate to Rollitt
1961-1971

During 1961/62, Mike Ellery swept past Reg Quick's record of tries scored in a season. Quick's total of 33 was set in 1920/21, but Ellery eclipsed this with 44, which is still the Bristol record and is likely to remain so, as far fewer games are played in the professional era. Here, Ellery and Quick share a beer in the Hole in the Wall pub in Redcliffe to celebrate the breaking of Quick's record.

Derek Neate succeeded Blake as captain in 1961/62, and was able to lead his team on a much improved Memorial Ground surface, following work done in the summer. At the same time, new posts were erected and, at 56ft, they were certainly the tallest posts in the country, and possibly even the world, at that time. Bristol achieved a reasonable record of 28 wins, saving their best display for another visit to Ninian Park, where Cardiff were beaten 20-3. Part of this game was televised, and Bristol played some dazzling rugby, despite being reduced to thirteen men due to injuries.

J.D. Thorne became Bristol's regular hooker, shortly after the retirement of Don Woodward in 1956. He featured in England trials from 1957, and was eventually capped 3 times in 1963. His first international, England's 13-6 victory over Wales was England's last win in Cardiff for twenty-eight years. John Thorne joined Bristol from Cleve, and appeared for Gloucestershire in the 1959 county final. The programme notes for the final said of Thorne: '...charges around like a rhino in the loose; strikes like an adder in the tight.' John Thorne was a member of England's first overseas tour party to New Zealand and Australia in 1963. He returned to Cleve in the mid-1960s, but helped out Bristol in 1972, to complete 287 matches for the club. He also played once for Newport. His voice was heard on the Memorial Ground tannoy for many years.

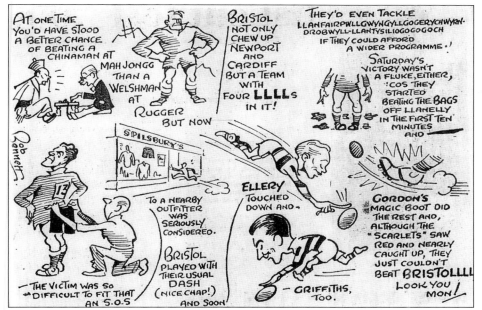

Bob Bennett's sporting cartoons were a popular feature in the local press for many years. This example celebrates a Bristol victory over Llanelli during the Blake era, and pokes gentle fun at the Welsh use of the 'll' sound. It is interesting to see that a player is shown running to Spilsbury's outfitters. Charlie Spilsbury played for Bristol before the Second World War, and his clothes shop was on Gloucester Road, close to the Bristol ground. Bob Bennett's son, Roger, can regularly be heard on Radio Bristol.

The club celebrated its seventy-fifth anniversary in 1962/63. Under Derek Neate's captaincy, only 10 games were lost, but the dreadful winter of 1963 saw the cancellation of all rugby from Boxing Day until mid-February. When play eventually resumed, Bristol enjoyed an unbeaten run of 8 matches, including a welcome victory over Cardiff. From left to right, back row: J.D. Currie, R.V. Bridgeman, J. Glover, T.A.B. Mahoney, J.D. Thorne, M.L. Lawrence, A. Davies. Middle row: P.J. Williams (secretary), A.J. Weaver, M.R. Collins, D.J. Spratt, J.V. Pullin, D.J.S. Mann, J.N. Blake, C.M. Hollister, J.R.D. Morris, A.R. Northover (treasurer). Front row: P.L.E. Storkey, L. Davies, D.J. Weeks, D.W. Neate (captain), C.R. Setter (president), P.J. Colston, D. St G. Hazell, R.V. Grove, J.R.E. Bryan (chairman).

Various special events were held during the season. Journalist Horace Hutt updated the history he had first prepared for the fiftieth anniversary, and there was a special service in St Stephen's church in the city. A celebration banquet was held, and Bristol played a commemorative game against J.T.W. Berry's International XV. Unfortunately, rain spoiled this match, which the International XV (largely the England side which was to tour New Zealand and Australia) won 3-0. The informative programme is shown here.

Bristol also staged a special seventy-fifth anniversary Sevens tournament, inviting the likes of Harlequins, Bath, Gloucester and Wasps to the Memorial Ground on 21 October. Bristol had a splendid day, eventually winning their own tournament with a 21-8 victory over Cheltenham in the final. This is the tournament programme.

One of the best performances of the season was, in fact, a defeat. Trailing Newport at half time, in a special floodlit game in October, Bristol played superbly in the second half and nearly snatched the game. Only the fact that they dropped a potential scoring pass at the end denied them victory. The club received a letter from a Newport supporter afterwards, stating: 'I have played and watched rugby for many years and I can honestly say that the second half was some of the most exciting football I have seen.' The illustration shows the programme for this honourable 18-16 defeat.

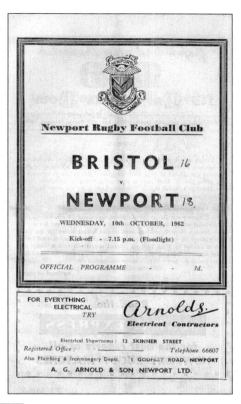

Newport Rugby Football Club

BRISTOL *16*

v.

NEWPORT *18*

WEDNESDAY, 10th OCTOBER, 1962

Kick-off - 7.15 p.m. (Floodlight)

OFFICIAL PROGRAMME - - 3d.

FOR EVERYTHING
ELECTRICAL
TRY *Arnolds*
Electrical Contractors

Electrical Showrooms : 13 SKINNER STREET
Registered Office :   *Telephone 66607*
Also Plumbing & Ironmongery Depts. 1 GODFREY ROAD, NEWPORT
A. G. ARNOLD & SON NEWPORT LTD.

Cornishman Jim Glover gained Oxford blues in 1959 and 1960 as a winger, captaining his university in the latter game. He joined Bristol in 1961, making 199 appearances in all, mainly as a centre. Jim Glover also captained Cornwall and played for the Barbarians.

Full-back P.J. Colston took over the Bristol captaincy from Derek Neate in 1963/64. Peter Colston joined the club from St Brendan's Old Boys in 1957, and played 252 games in a distinguished career, which included appearances for both Gloucestershire and Somerset, as well as the Western Counties team v. New Zealand in 1963. After retiring due to a back injury, he was invited to become the club's first coach in 1969. His expertise in this position was rewarded with Bristol's best ever season in 1971/72, and he went on to coach England in the mid-1970s, later serving as Bristol's chairman.

Having experimented for some years with floodlit rugby, Bristol finally unveiled their own lights in October 1963. Cardiff, so often the club's guests for important occasions, were defeated 12-6. There was still a reluctance to count floodlit fixtures in the official records, and such games remained unofficial until 1965/66. The 1963/64 season, as a whole, saw 28 victories from 45 games. This is the special programme for the switching on of the floodlights.

RUGBY UNION FOOTBALL UNDER FLOODLIGHTS

THE INAUGURAL MATCH
FOR THE NEW FLOODLIGHTING SYSTEM

BRISTOL

v

CARDIFF

AT THE

MEMORIAL GROUND, FILTON AVENUE

ON

THURSDAY, OCTOBER 24TH, 1963

Kick Off 7.30 p.m.

— : : —

THERE WILL BE A SWITCHING-ON CEREMONY AT 7.25 p.m.

— : : —

PROGRAMME 3d.

B.W. Redwood formed an appealing partnership with John Blake at half back in the late 1950s, and is recognized as one of the club's truly great players. Scandalously neglected by the England selectors for many years, Bill Redwood eventually gained 2 caps at scrum-half in 1968, scoring a try on his debut against Wales. Capable of turning the course of a game through his innovative genius, he played 243 Bristol matches, scoring 433 points. He missed out on a blue during a brief spell at Oxford University, but he was a regular for Gloucestershire and captained Bristol from 1967-69. Bill Redwood, who learnt his rugby at Bristol Grammar School, achieved greatness on the rugby field, despite having only one effective eye. His father, Percy, and brother, Bob, also played for the club.

The 1964/65 season, Peter Colston's second as captain, was a disappointment. Bristol were hindered by injuries to Colston himself, as well as to vice-captain, John Thorne. 18 games were lost, and only 3 won out of the last 11. However, Swansea were beaten twice and floodlit rugby proved popular. From left to right, back row: P.J. Williams (secretary), D.J. Spratt, J.V. Pullin, D.W. Neate, D.E.J. Watt, T.A.B. Mahoney, P.R. Cowles, J. Szyszkiewicz, A.J. Rogers, G.G. White, J.R.E. Bryan (chairman). Front row: D.J. Weeks, M.G. Ellery, J. Glover, P.J. Colston (captain), C.R. Setter (president), J.D. Thorne, M.R. Collins, D.A. Phillips, R.C. Wallace.

Derek Neate returned to captain Bristol in 1965/66, and led the club to a superb record of 39 wins from 47 matches. No Bristol team has ever won so many games in a season, although the great 1971/72 side equalled this total. Only Cardiff and Liverpool won at Bristol, and there were doubles over Bath, Harlequins and Leicester. Bristol became champions of the unofficial *Sunday Telegraph* English merit table during this season. From left to right, back row: J.V. Pullin, J.V. Coles, T.E. Base, T.A.B. Mahoney, B.W. Redwood, R.C. Wallace. Middle row: A.R. Northover (treasurer), P.L.E. Storkey, D.A. Phillips, D.M. Rollitt, N.R. Mayne, D.E.J. Watt, P.R. Cowles, H.A. Hill, R.V. Grove, J. Wilson, P.J. Williams (secretary). Front row: M.R. Collins, M.G. Ellery, J.R.E. Bryan (chairman), D.W. Neate (captain), C.R. Setter (president), P.J. Colston, P.R. Hillard, B. Perry.

Bristol's first home game of the 1965/66 season was a spectacular affair against a strong Northampton side. Trailing 16-5 at half-time, Bristol staged a remarkable second-half recovery to win 18-16. In all, Bristol scored four tries, the winner coming in the dying seconds from teenage centre Peter Hillard, who beat four players on his way to the posts. Here, Hillard draws the Northampton full-back, before passing to the long-striding Mike Ellery on the wing. Between Hillard and Ellery, is the partially-obscured Bristol centre, Alan Watson, and a worried-looking Andy Hancock, Northampton's England international wing. Peter Hillard played for Bristol between 1964 and 1970, making his debut as an eighteen year old. His blistering pace, honed by sprinting training with Westbury Harriers, helped him cross for 32 tries for Bristol. He also represented Gloucestershire. Injury-prone, he left Bristol to pursue a career in computers, and he later played international rugby for Zambia and Jamaica.

P.J. Williams, a forward, played 146 games for Bristol in the years after the First World War. He also played for Gloucestershire, and was largely responsible for organizing the Bristol Supporters' Team during the Second World War. Percy Williams became Bristol's honorary general secretary in 1949, and held this office until his retirement in 1966. In his final annual report for the club, he wrote: 'I shall leave with the thought that I always worked with one object in view and that was the success of the Bristol Football Club, to me the finest club in the country.' An honorary life member of the club since 1954, Percy Williams died in 1983.

1966/67 saw an incredible 55 first-team fixtures, of which 38 were won. Captain Derek Neate was ill for much of the season, but four Bristol players gained England caps, and there were good wins over Newport, Bridgend and a double over Gloucester. From left to right, back row: J.V. Coles, G.W. Morris, A.D. Watson, J.V. Pullin, D. Woodward. Middle row: P.L.E. Storkey, D.H. Taylor, A.H. Nicholls, B.G. Nelmes, B.A. Dovey, D.M. Rollitt, K.E. Miller, N.R. Mayne, P.R. Cowles, H.A. Hill, J.R.E. Bryan (chairman), T.A.B. Mahoney. Front row: A.J. Rogers, D.E.J. Watt, B.W. Redwood, C.R. Setter (president), D.W. Neate (captain), M.R. Collins, R. Dunn.

R.W. Hosen, a Cornishman, joined Bristol in 1966, and scored 259 points in 48 games. A full-back, Roger Hosen gained the first of his 10 England caps as a Northampton player on England's tour to New Zealand in 1963. He was so impressive on this tour that he was named a Player of the Year by the *Rugby Almanac* of New Zealand. One newspaper was moved to pose the question: 'Who's this New Zealander playing full-back for England?' A noted goal kicker, Hosen joined Bristol when his teaching duties took him to Cheltenham College, and he gained his last 5 caps as a Bristol player. His record of 38 points in the 1966/67 international championship stood until 1979. A noted cricketer, a Cornish newspaper named him in its greatest ever Cornish Cricket XI.

R.A.W. Sharp, one of rugby's immortals, played 31 Bristol games from 1964-67. A speedy fly-half with a superb sidestep, Richard Sharp played 14 games for England, gaining his final cap from the Bristol club in 1967, when he captained his country against Australia. A Cornishman, he represented his county and also played for Redruth, Wasps and the Barbarians. He gained 3 blues at Oxford and toured South Africa with the 1962 British Lions. He later became a regular contributor to *The Sunday Telegraph*'s rugby pages.

Hooker J.V. Pullin, one of the outstanding figures in the club's history, made his debut in 1961, and played 296 games up to 1978. A superb striker of the ball in the scrum, John Pullin, who was educated at Thornbury Grammar School and joined the club from Bristol Saracens, gained a total of 42 England caps. This was a record eventually exceeded by Tony Neary in 1980. A farmer, he captained his country on 13 occasions, including victories over South Africa, New Zealand and Australia. He also played for Gloucestershire, and one of his many games for the Barbarians was the famous 1973 victory over New Zealand. John Pullin toured with the 1968 and 1971 British Lions, appearing in 7 Test matches.

BRISTOL FOOTBALL CLUB
(RUGBY FOOTBALL UNION)

CORNISH TOUR
1967

APRIL 22nd — 25th

Matches versus

PLYMOUTH ALBION
CAMBORNE — REDRUTH

HEADQUARTERS
CLIFFDENE HOTEL, NEWQUAY
Tel. Nos.
Newquay 3094 (Management)
3095 (Visitors)

Captain: D. W. NEATE
Vice-Captain: B. W. REDWOOD
Hon. Team Sec 1st XV: D. H. TAYLOR

Bristol toured Devon and Cornwall in April 1967, defeating Plymouth Albion (11-8), Camborne (6-3) and Redruth (20-3). The tour itinerary, shown here, includes the following warning: 'It is essential that the high standard of behaviour already shown during this season be maintained. Should any unruly behaviour occur, it will result in those concerned being asked to leave the hotel, and they will be personally responsible for any damage done.'

D.E.J. Watt, one of Bristol's greatest ever forwards, played 512 matches, as a number eight and second row, between 1958 and 1975. Initially a soccer player, David Watt was attracted to rugby by its social life, and played a handful of games for St Mary's Old Boys and Bristol Harlequins. Despite originally having been selected for a Welsh trial, he chose to play for England, and appeared in 4 internationals in 1967. He toured with England to Canada in 1967 and South Africa in 1972. He captained Gloucestershire in 1971/72, and led the Western Counties side that played New Zealand at Gloucester in 1972. At the end of his career, he also represented Somerset. A huge man, his was the largest ever measure for a Bristol blazer. Dave Watt scored 52 tries for the club and served on the Bristol committee for nine years after retiring from playing.

Prop forward, B.A. Dovey, made his England debut alongside John Thorne in 1963, as a Rosslyn Park player. He joined Bristol in 1965, and made 184 appearances up to 1970. He was Bristol's vice-captain in the 1967/68 season. Bev Dovey, who was twice capped by England, played at various times for Gloucestershire, Hertfordshire and Yorkshire. He was a Cambridge blue in 1960 and also played for the Barbarians.

J.D. Currie, a second-row forward, gained four rugby blues at Oxford University and already had 22 England caps when a job with W.D. & H.O. Wills brought him back to Bristol, the city of his birth. A Harlequins player, he appeared in England's Grand Slam team of 1957 and formed a highly-respected second-row partnership with David Marques. He joined Bristol on his return to the city, and gained a further 3 England caps in 1962. John Currie, who attended Bristol Grammar School, played county rugby for both Gloucestershire and Somerset, and appeared in one first-class cricket match for Somerset. He died in 1990.

Bill Redwood's 1967/68 team was greatly disrupted by injury, and lost 18 games. The team was, however, undefeated in London, and gained a notable 11-9 victory at Richmond, on a day when Gloucestershire were playing Somerset in the county championship, thus depriving the side of virtually all of its first-choice players. From left to right, back row: D.G. Tyler, J.S. Marsh, J. Glover. Second row: T.A.B. Mahoney (secretary), A.R. Northover (treasurer), N.R. Mayne, A.M. Pearce, D.E.J. Watt, P.R. Cowles, A.J. Hoon, P.A.L. Williams, R.G. Frame, P.L.E. Storkey, J.R.E. Bryan (chairman). Third row: D.M. Rollitt, D. Impey, C.R. Setter (president), B.W. Redwood (captain), A.J. Rogers, J.V. Pullin. Front row: A.H. Nicholls, J.V. Coles, P.R. Hillard, M.R. Collins.

Bill Redwood's second season of captaincy saw Bristol achieve 30 wins from 51 games. A record 597 points were conceded, which suggests that defence was the club's Achilles heel. Redwood himself was only able to play 10 games, due to injury, and his distinguished career came to an end that season. Bristol's excellent 19-16 victory over Harlequins at Twickenham in November 1968 was almost entirely due to a half-hour of brilliance from Redwood.

Bristol's Easter Monday game with Northampton in April 1969 brought a welcome 33-11 victory. Here, scrum-half J.D. Perkins, Bill Redwood's stand-in for many games during the season, sends out a dive pass, watched by number eight forward, Neil Tye. David Perkins, a popular teacher and rugby coach at Queen Elizabeth's Hospital School in Bristol for many years, played 41 games for the club.

Speedy winger, M.R. Collins, played 303 games for the club from 1961-1971, scoring 146 tries. Always a favourite with the Bristol crowd, Mike Collins played 46 games for Gloucestershire and represented Western Counties against New Zealand in 1963, Australia in 1967, South Africa in 1969 and Fiji in 1970. He also played for the South of England against New Zealand in 1967. Mike Collins, a product of the Bristol Saracens, where he started as a flanker, is seen here (right) opposing Bath's England winger, Peter Glover, during Bristol's 32-6 win at Bath in April 1971. Shortly afterwards, his job took him away from Bristol and he joined Rosslyn Park.

Yorkshireman D.M. Rollitt came to Bristol University in 1961 and, after a spell at Loughborough Colleges, returned to the city to take up a teaching post at Colston's School. A flanker or number eight forward, David Rollitt was a popular Bristol player for many years, making a total of 415 appearances up to 1977, scoring 102 tries. His prematurely grey hair made him a distinctive figure on the rugby stage, and he is regarded as one of the club's greatest ever forwards. David Rollitt captained Bristol from 1969-71, and gained 11 England caps, a scandalously small number in a career stretching from 1967 to 1975. He captained Gloucestershire and appeared regularly against touring sides, captaining Western Counties against South Africa in 1969 and Fiji in 1970. His son, Eben, also played for the club.

Back-row forward, D.A. Phillips, made 204 appearances for Bristol, in a career lasting from 1963 to 1975. An England Schools' international, David Phillips first played for the club as an eighteen year old, and made his Somerset debut at the age of twenty. A product of the Bishopston Club, he trained at St Luke's College, Exeter, and was often unavailable for Bristol during his student years. He became a regular in the team in the 1970/71 season. David Phillips was noted for his speed and for the strength of his tackling.

A.H. Nicholls made his Bristol debut against Gloucester in 1966, dropping a goal within minutes of taking the field. Tony Nicholls was a centre on that occasion, but played the bulk of his rugby at outside half, including in England trials in 1966. He became captain of Bristol in 1971/72, and led the club for three seasons. His calm, yet inspirational, style of leadership was a huge success, and he deservedly ranks among the best of the club's captains. His excellent understanding with Alan Pearn at half-back was one of the main reasons for Bristol's high quality play in the early 1970s. Schoolteacher Tony Nicholls, who also played county rugby for Sussex, made 311 Bristol appearances, scoring 775 points.

The 1969/70 season, the first under the leadership of David Rollitt, saw 32 wins out of 51 games played. There were notable victories home and away over Swansea, Pontypool and Harlequins, and the team scored 908 points and 188 tries, both new records. Peter Colston was appointed as the club's first coach and this, together with the arrival of several new players, paved the way for the improvement in fortunes. Back row: K.C. Plummer, J.R. White, K.E. Miller, P. Gunter, S. Millard. Middle Row: T.A.B. Mahoney (secretary), R.R. Morris (committee), J.P. Luff, J.V. Pullin, B.G. Nelmes, D.E.J. Watt, M. McKenzie, A.J. Rogers, D.G. Tyler, E. Trumbell, J.R.E. Bryan (chairman) Front row: R.J. Williams, B.A. Dovey, D.M. Rollitt (captain), C.R. Setter (president), A.H. Nicholls, A.J.G. Morley, M.R. Collins.

In 1969, Bristol and an Edinburgh District XV were invited to Clermont-Ferrand by the French regional committee to play in an Armistice rugby tournament. The first game, against ASM Clermont-Ferrand, was a brutal match. Bristol had been entertained before the encounter and tempted with an excess of wine. Although consumption was moderate, Rollitt's team were not prepared to put up with illegal French tactics and indifferent refereeing during the game. At one point, there was a twenty-eight-man fight, with only Alan Morley and his opposite wing not involved. The incensed Rollitt took the team off the pitch, but they were persuaded to return, only to lose 13-3. In their second game, against the Auvergne province, there were few unsavoury incidents. Bristol lost 24-17, but pride was restored.

AUVERGNE

FER

Journées
Internationales
du Comité
d'Auvergne

CLERMONT-FERRAND, les 9 et 11 Novembre 1969

prix :
2 f.

PROGRAMME OFFICIEL
Avec tirage de la bourriche

R.C. Hannaford, a number eight forward, played 108 Bristol matches from 1970-74, and won 3 caps for England in 1971, scoring a try on his debut against Wales. A Cambridge blue in 1967, he played for Durham and Gloucestershire, and later worked in New Zealand. Charlie Hannaford, shown in his England shirt, joined Bristol when he became a master at Clifton College, and was a member of the Gloucestershire team that, in 1972, won the county championship, for the first time since 1937. He also played for Gloucester and Rosslyn Park.

1970/71, David Rollitt's second season in charge, was something of a disappointment, with only 29 games being won out of 50 played. There were, however, good home wins over Newport, Cardiff and Northampton. The Cardiff victory, on a Friday evening in February, was Bristol's first in the fixture since 1963. Despite the absence of John Pullin and Charlie Hannaford (both away on England duty), Bristol bounced back from a run of three defeats to score an entertaining 13-6 victory. The illustration shows referee P.R. Johnson of London about to award a penalty. On the ground, is Bristol scrum-half, David Perkins, who enjoyed his tussle with the great Gareth Edwards, rear left.

Cornish winger, K.C. Plummer, scored 139 tries in 269 games for Bristol, having previously played for Penryn. He made his England debut against Wales in 1969 and was recalled for a further 3 caps in 1976. Ken Plummer played 52 games for Cornwall and represented South-West Counties against Australia, Fiji, New Zealand and South Africa, as well as playing for the Barbarians. He captained Bristol from 1976-78, after which a shoulder injury finished this speedy and exciting winger's career.

P.M. Knight, who was educated at Bristol Cathedral School, played for Bristol United as a sixteen-year-old, and returned to play for the club after his time at Durham University and St Luke's College, Exeter. A highly gifted winger and full-back, Peter Knight scored 51 tries in 102 Bristol matches, and gained 3 England caps in 1972. He appeared as a full-back against France and Scotland and as a winger in England's famous victory in South Africa. Peter Knight, who is now a clergyman, played in 3 county finals for Gloucestershire, and was a brilliant sevens player. He retired prematurely from rugby in 1974.

A.J.G. Morley, a three-quarter, played for Bristol from 1969 to 1986. A prolific try-scorer, Alan Morley set new records for the club, playing in 519 matches for the First XV and scoring 384 tries. In total, he scored 479 tries in first-class rugby, a world record. His total of 1516 points for Bristol included 4 conversions and a dropped goal. Unusually for a Bristolian in the side, he had no true affiliation with a local club, having first played for Bristol United whilst at Colston's School, although he did play for Old Colstonians on a handful of occasions. He captained Bristol from 1980-1982.

Alan Morley was approached to play for Wales, qualifying through his Welsh mother but he declined, and played for England on seven occasions. He made his debut against South Africa in Johannesburg in 1972 and scored the only try of the match, which England won 18-9. In 1974, he was called up as a replacement for the British Lions in South Africa. He represented Gloucestershire on 73 occasions, scoring tries in the county championship final victories of 1983 and 1984. He also played for the Barbarians. Alan Morley was awarded the MBE for services to rugby in the Queen's Birthday Honours list of 1985, as seen in this picture. He retired at the end of Bristol's tour to Canada in 1986.

Four

Triumphs of the Seventies

1971-1980

Bristol's 1971/72 team remains, arguably, the greatest in the history of the club. Under Tony Nicholls's leadership, they won a record-equalling 39 games, losing 7 and drawing 3. Aided by the increase of the value of a try to 4 points, the side scored 1,145 points, easily a new record. Nicholls, who played in all 49 games, and his coach, Peter Colston, encouraged open rugby, and Bristol scored 177 tries. The club won both the *Sunday Telegraph* English merit table, and the table for English and Welsh clubs, courtesy of Alan Pearn's last-minute drop goal in the final match of the season at Pontypool. From left to right, back row: A.L. Cornish, A.F.A. Pearn, R.J. Orledge, R.C. Hannaford, A.J. Rogers, J.P. Luff, D.G. Tyler, R.D.H. Bryce, K.C. Plummer, P.J. Colston (coach). Front row: D.M. Rollitt, J.R. White, A.H. Nicholls, J.R. Gabitass, R.L. Swaffield, N.D. Evans, D.A. Phillips.

A.F.A. Pearn, a scrum-half from Devon, joined Bristol from St Luke's College, Exeter, in 1970, when he gained a teaching job in the area. Bristol did not have a regular goal kicker at the time, and Alan Pearn was asked to take on the kicking duties. He had the ability to kick goals from any part of the opposition's territory, and possessed a remarkable pass, being able to locate players over half the width of the pitch away with pinpoint accuracy. He broke Gordon Cripps's old club record in 1971/72 by scoring 429 points, and extended this to 452 the following season. Altogether, he scored 2,047 points for Bristol, a record only beaten in later years by Mark Tainton. Alan Pearn played many games for Devon, but his adventurous scrum-half play was cruelly ignored by England, although he was on the England replacements bench in 1971. He made 286 appearances for Bristol between 1970 and 1979, scoring 67 tries.

CARDIFF ARMS PARK

CARDIFF RUGBY CLUB

SEASON 1971 - 1972

—

CARDIFF

v

BRISTOL

—

THURSDAY, 10th FEBRUARY, 1972

KICK OFF 7.15 P.M.

OFFICIAL PROGRAMME

PRICE 4 PENCE

PROVINCIAL PRINTING AND PUBLISHING CO., LTD., FERRY ROAD, CARDIFF

So many of the 1971/72 games are noteworthy. Newport were defeated 41-19 in early September, and Bristol followed this with a 38-4 win at Swansea. Excellent victories were recorded at Richmond and London Scottish, on days when Gloucestershire players were unavailable, and there was a classic 24-19 home win over Coventry. Best of all, Bristol won at Cardiff for the first time in thirty-nine years, on a night when Dave Watt broke the Bristol appearance record. This is the programme for Bristol's historic 15-12 win.

In March 1972, Plymouth Albion travelled to play a strong Bristol team, during the evening of an international Saturday. It was a journey they made with some trepidation. Their fears became reality, when Bristol clocked up a remarkable 84-6 victory. Bristol scored sixteen tries, five of them coming from Alan Morley. Centre Chris Williams tore the Plymouth defence to shreds, created several tries and scored three himself. Alan Pearn converted ten of the tries, and contributed twenty-four points in all. Plymouth battled valiantly to keep out the relentless waves of Bristol attacks, and were forced to play with thirteen players, due to injury, for the majority of the match. Here, Morley races away for one of his tries, pursued in vain by the Plymouth defence.

Bristol United in 1971/72, under the captaincy of Gloucestershire cricketer, David Green, played 35 matches, winning 23, drawing 2 and losing 10. The team achieved some high-scoring victories, including 51-6 at Crumlin, 60-7 at Camberley, and 64-0 at home to Cinderford. From left to right, back row: J. Trott, D.P. Power, J.R.E. Bryan (chairman), P.H. Wylie, K.R. Phelps, B.J. Morrison, D.M. Green, J.P. Luff, S.J. Tilley, K.R. Beeton, A.P. Ramsey, M.J. Rhodes, J.S. Marsh (treasurer), T.A.B. Mahoney (secretary). Middle row: M.J. Fry, R.L. Swaffield, P.R. Sams, C.R. Setter (president), A.C. Munden, S.G. Crabtree, D.A. Phillips. Front row: R.J. Kays, P.M. Smith.

RUGBY FOOTBALL UNION

BRISTOL

v

COVENTRY

CLUB COMPETITION FINAL

Twickenham
Saturday
28th April 1973

Official Programme
Price **10p**

1972/73 was not quite as good as the previous season, 18 games being lost. Bristol did, however, reach their first knock-out cup final, a competition which the RFU had introduced in 1971/72. Bristol won a thrilling semi-final at London Welsh, coming back from a 15-3 deficit. Such was the home side's dominance in the first half, that a premature tannoy announcement was made at half time concerning tickets for the final. This acted as a spur for Bristol, who eventually won 18-15, and thus went through to the final against Coventry at Twickenham. This is the programme for the final – a very plain publication in those pre-sponsorship days.

Bristol's colours were very similar to Coventry's, so they wore white shirts when the teams met in the final. Winger Ken Plummer was unable to play, due to injury, so Mike Dandy was called up to make a rare first-team appearance. This picture shows the Bristol team, before its encounter with a Coventry side containing eleven internationals. From left to right, back row: A.F.A. Pearn, D.M. Rollitt, D.E.J. Watt, R.J. Orledge, R.C. Hannaford, A.J. Rogers, M.J. Fry, P.M. Knight, A.C. Munden. Front row: C.J. Williams, J.V. Pullin, R.L. Swaffield, A.H. Nicholls (captain), A.J.G. Morley, M.J.W. Dandy.

Bristol's chances of a Twickenham victory were dashed in the very first minute, when hooker John Pullin was stretchered off with torn knee ligaments. Ridiculously, no replacements were allowed, so Bristol fought bravely with fourteen men for the rest of the game, eventually going down 27-15. Alan Pearn, who scored all his side's points from five penalty goals, is shown here sending out a dive pass. Note the many empty seats – early cup finals were not well attended.

Few Bristol captains have had their term in office extended beyond two seasons, but Tony Nicholls was deservedly elected for a third season of leadership. Back to their best, Bristol were again *Sunday Telegraph* English Champions, and won 35 games out of 49. Bristol won another cup match at London Welsh, and gained double victories over Bath, Harlequins, Newbridge, Northampton, and Swansea. From left to right, back row: D.M. Rollitt, K.C. Plummer, D.A. Phillips, M.J. Fry, A.J. Rogers, D.G. Tyler, R.S. Carter, S.J. Gorvett. Middle row: J.R.E. Bryan (chairman), T.A.B. Mahoney (secretary), A.C. Munden, M. Hannell, R.J. Orledge, P.R. Sams, D.P. Sorrell, P.L. Waters, R.L. Swaffield, A.J. Hignell, J.S. Marsh (treasurer), A.L. Cornish. Front row: A.P. Ramsey, A.F.A. Pearn, D.E.J. Watt, J.R. White, C.R. Setter (president), A.H. Nicholls (captain), D. Woodward, C.J. Williams, P.M. Knight.

Farming and representative rugby frequently took John Pullin away from the Bristol team, but, fortunately, the club was able to call on the not inconsiderable hooking talents of J.R. White. Described by no less an authority than Dave Watt as 'a line-out forward's dream', John White was renowned for his skill as a thrower-in, as well as for his contributions in open play. He was good enough to go to New Zealand as Pullin's number two when England toured in 1973, although he never won a cap. Such was White's popularity, that his team mates wanted to elect him as Bristol captain when Tony Nicholls stood down after the 1973/74 season. When their intentions were made known John Pullin, realizing that he would no longer be guaranteed a first-team place, hinted that he might have to look elsewhere for his rugby. Rather than cause a problem, White put club before self and withdrew his nomination. John 'Chalky' White played 221 Bristol games between 1967 and 1976.

Following White's withdrawal, D.G. Tyler was appointed captain for 1974/75. A popular and long-serving player, David Tyler was a centre at Bristol Grammar School and played his early rugby for Bristol as either a centre or wing, gaining an England trial in 1967. He later converted to full-back, and played a grand total of 425 first-team games, scoring 154 tries. He appeared regularly for Somerset and played against various touring teams. After his retirement as a player, David Tyler coached Bristol's 1983 cup-winning team and later worked professionally for Bristol as an administrator.

1974/75 was not a successful season, with Bristol losing 22 games. The side was often disrupted by representative calls and consequently struggled to find consistent form. One of the few highlights of the season was Dave Watt's 500th appearance for the club. The match itself, a 13-3 home cup defeat against Gosforth, was something of an anticlimax, but the achievement was marked by a special dinner dance, and Watt was made an honorary vice-president. The illustration shows the dinner dance menu.

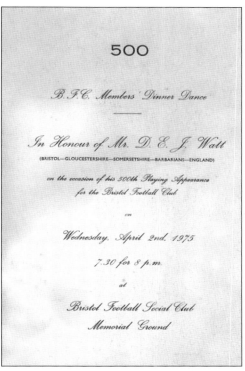

500

B.F.C. Members' Dinner Dance

In Honour of Mr. D. E. J. Watt
(BRISTOL—GLOUCESTERSHIRE—SOMERSETSHIRE—BARBARIANS—ENGLAND)

*on the occasion of his 500th Playing Appearance
for the Bristol Football Club*

on

Wednesday, April 2nd, 1975

7.30 for 8 p.m.

at

*Bristol Football Social Club
Memorial Ground*

1975/76, David Tyler's second season as captain, saw the team back to its best. 37 games were won and 1,054 points scored. The team really hit form following a disappointing 16-12 home cup quarter-final defeat against Rosslyn Park. The following Wednesday, Bristol travelled to Pontypool to face a formidable pack, including the legendary 'Pontypool Front Row' of Charlie Faulkner, Bobby Windsor and Graham Price, plus star flanker and captain Terry Cobner. Bristol stunned their hosts, winning 34-8, the first of a 12-match winning streak. This picture shows action from Bristol's December home game with Llanelli. Skipper Tyler is pictured here, scoring a try in the first minute of Bristol's 16-3 victory. The other Bristol player is Mike Hussey, while the Llanelli player is Welsh international and British Lion wing, J.J. Williams.

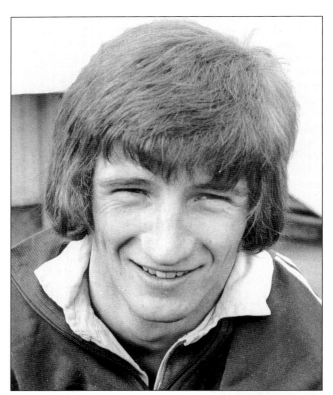

C.J. Williams made his Bristol debut as a nineteen-year-old full-back on the sacred turf of Twickenham, against Harlequins in 1970. Chris Williams played a total of 310 games for the club, mainly as a centre, scoring 60 tries. Renowned for his fierce tackling, he suffered a badly broken leg at Swansea in 1977 but, to the delight of many Bristol supporters, he battled back to fitness, playing his final first-team game in 1983. He joined the club from Bristol Combination club Aretians, and returned to them at the end of his Bristol career. An England Schools' cap at under-16 level, Chris Williams played many times for Gloucestershire, and later coached the County XV.

R.S. Carter, a winger from Weston-Super-Mare, made his Bristol debut in 1973, and scored 92 tries in his 220 appearances for the club. Robbie Carter played for the Hornets club in Weston, and was noted for his fearless tackling and his speed. He played county rugby for Somerset, and appeared for Western Counties against Australia in 1975.

1976/77 saw the appointment of Ken Plummer as captain. Again, the side was disrupted by representative calls, and there were many injuries to key players. In all, the club lost 19 games. At the end of the season, a short tour of France saw a welcome return to form, with 2 wins out of 3 matches. The visit of Richmond on Friday 18 February was unusual in that the game kicked off at 9.05 p.m., because the visiting team was delayed by heavy traffic. Bristol rewarded their patient supporters with five tries in a 23-6 victory, and replacement Phil Cue achieved the unique distinction of joining the action at 9.50 p.m.

№ 213

BRISTOL FOOTBALL CLUB
(RUGBY FOOTBALL UNION)

BRISTOL
v
RICHMOND

Memorial Ground, Filton Avenue

FRIDAY   18th. FEBRUARY   1977

Kick Off   7.30 p.m.

PROGRAMME   10p

**You can always trust Target
to be on the ball**

For Life Assurance Endowment Mortgages and Your Financial Needs Consult.

TARGET TRUST GROUP
TARGET HOUSE
33/37 BROADMEAD, BRISTOL
Telephone: 25381

The tradition of Bristol rugby players excelling at cricket dates back to pre-war times, when the Bristol Rugbeians had a regular fixture list. This photograph, from 1974, shows the team that won the Knowle six-a-side tournament. One of the six, David Green, was a successful first-class cricketer for Lancashire and Gloucestershire, and is now a prominent sports journalist. Alan Ramsey, a prop forward, had his playing career cut short due to a serious neck injury, but served on the committee for many years, eventually becoming chairman. David Woodward, a second-row forward, would have played far more than his 117 Bristol games, but for injury. He played regular county rugby for Somerset. The photograph shows, from left to right: Tony Nicholls, Alan Ramsey, David Woodward, David Tyler, David Green, Peter Colston.

1977/78 was another season in which Bristol found it difficult to field a settled side. 16 games were lost, and captain Ken Plummer was forced to retire halfway through the season. At that time, qualification for the knock-out cup was based on performances in regional merit tables. A careless defeat at Exeter in April meant that Bristol failed to qualify for the following season's competition. From left to right, back row: M.J. Pegler, C.J. Williams, M.L. Baker, D.L. Chidgey, S. Woolway, N.J.C. Pomphrey, N. Gaymond, A.H. Troughton, A. Sheppard, M.C. Caven, A.J.G. Morley, M.J. Fry, D. Impey. Middle row: E.E. Burridge (chairman), T.A.B. Mahoney (secretary), J. Tasker, M. Rafter, J.R.E. Bryan (president), K.C. Plummer (captain), J. Lane, J. Kelly, A.L. Cornish. Front row: P.J. Polledri, A.F.A. Pearn.

On 16 April 1978, Bristol played a game of Socby against Bristol City Football Club, as part of local physiotherapist Les Bardsley's testimonial year. At the time, he was physiotherapist for both clubs. The Socby on this occasion was an eleven-a-side game. This photograph shows both the teams, prior to the match.

Bristol looked to be heading for another mediocre playing record in 1978/79 and, by early February, Mike Fry's team had already lost 12 games. The side then embarked on a superb run of 17 consecutive victories, which carried them right up to the end of the season. Young second-row forward, Nigel Pomphrey, scored 22 tries, a record for a Bristol forward in one season, and fly-half, David Sorrell, finished with 201 points. Highlights included taking Liverpool's unbeaten record in the January snow, and a rare win at Cardiff, in a game which was stopped early in the second half, due to a frozen pitch. From left to right, back row: J. Kelly, K.M. Bogira, M.L. Baker, R.J. Hesford, P.J. Stiff, S.J. Gorvett, N.J.C. Pomphrey, A Sheppard, J. Watson, M.N. Ward, R.S. Carter. Middle row: T.A.B. Mahoney (secretary), A.J. Hignell, A.F.A. Pearn, D.P. Sorrell, J.R.E. Bryan (president), M.J. Fry (captain), A.J.G. Morley, R. Edwards, E.E. Burridge (chairman), A.L. Cornish. Front row: R.M. Harding, J. Lane.

M.J. Fry, an outstanding prop forward who joined Bristol from local club, Cotham Park, in 1967, was appointed captain for 1978/79. Mike Fry played in every first-team game during his two seasons of captaincy, and extended this run to 100 consecutive matches. A regular Somerset player, he played for the South and South West against New Zealand in 1979, and was considered by many to be unlucky not to have played for England. Mike Fry, universally known as 'The Greek', played 435 games for Bristol and later captained Old Redcliffians.

A.J. Hignell played his early Bristol rugby as a scrum-half, but switched to full-back at Cambridge University. He played 14 games for England, making his debut on the 1975 Australian tour. A rugby and cricket blue, Alistair Hignell scored 7 centuries for Gloucestershire, including one against the 1976 West Indian side. He played 58 matches for Bristol, scoring 208 points. After teaching for a while at Bristol Cathedral School, he moved into broadcasting as a sports commentator. He has recently won great admiration and support in his brave battle against multiple sclerosis.

1979/80 was another successful season, with 34 wins and 4 draws out of 49 games. The team scored 1,038 points, defeating Aberavon (54-3) and Bath (44-6). The illustration shows the programme from a superb game at Cardiff in September 1979. Trailing 17-9 in the dying minutes, with fly-half David Sorrell off the field injured, Bristol, inspired by Alistair Hignell as Sorrell's stand-in, scored two brilliant tries through Alan Morley and Dave Newman to draw 17-17, earning a standing ovation from an appreciative Arms Park crowd.

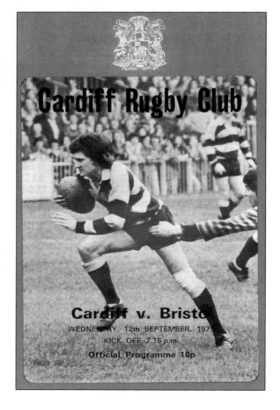

Five
The Quest for the Cup
1980-1984

N.J.C. Pomphrey, a player equally at home anywhere in the back five of the scrum, played for Bristol United whilst still at St Brendan's College. A powerful athlete, Nigel Pomphrey had a turn of speed more often seen in a three-quarter and, given the ball and a little space, he had the ability to score long-range tries from line-out or scrum. He made his debut against Gloucester as a second-row forward in September 1976, and was selected by the county side shortly afterwards. He was a replacement for England's match against USA in 1977, and toured the Far East with England in 1979, playing against Japan, Tonga and Fiji as a flank forward, at a time when caps were only awarded against major sides. Forced to choose between changing clubs to pursue an international career in the back row, or playing where Bristol needed him most in the second row, he displayed commendable loyalty and put club before self. He was selected for various invitation teams – England under-23 and 'B' XVs, as well as the Barbarians – but was never capped. He scored a record number of tries for a Bristol forward, 130, and played the last of his 364 games in the 1988 cup final. Nigel Pomphrey captained the club during their centenary season, an honour richly deserved by one of Bristol's most influential players.

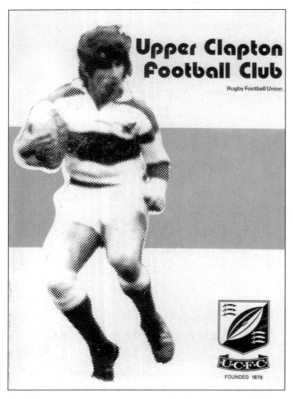

Upper Clapton Football Club

Rugby Football Union

U.C.F.C.

FOUNDED 1879

Alan Morley took over as captain for the 1980/81 season, but after a promising start the team's form fell away badly, culminating in an embarrassing occasion when a Bristol team containing four England players lost at home to Stroud. On 24 January, Bristol were warmly welcomed by junior Essex club, Upper Clapton, for a cup match which the visitors won 22-3. Eventual cup-winners, Leicester, knocked Bristol out in the following round, and the final playing record showed 30 wins, 2 draws and 18 defeats. This is the programme from the Upper Clapton game.

During the late 1960s, Bristol wisely decided to nurture local talent by running a regular Colts XV. This foresight paid dividends in future seasons, as a number of players groomed in colts rugby found a place in the senior side. One such player was D.P. Sorrell, who made his first-team debut in 1973, and went on to play 369 games. David Sorrell played chiefly as a fly-half, but could also play at centre or full-back. A talented kicker, he scored 1,699 points for Bristol. and played for Gloucestershire, England under-23 and England 'B', as well as appearing in an England trial. Sorrell, whose local club was Bishopston, was called out of retirement to play his final first-team game at Exeter in 1992.

92

R.M. Harding, a scrum-half, made his
Bristol debut at Leicester in
December 1973, along with David
Sorrell. Richard Harding, who won
two rugby blues at Cambridge, was
Bristol's regular scrum-half for much
of the 1980s, playing 395 games. A
Gloucestershire player, he made his
England debut against Romania in
1985, and captained his country in
the last of his 12 internationals on
tour in Fiji in 1988. He gained a
special place in rugby folklore when
his tackle on French winger Patrick
Esteve prevented a try, after the
player had crossed the line, thus
earning England a 9-9 draw at
Twickenham in 1985.

Lancastrian R.J. Hesford, a number eight forward,
played for Bristol from 1978 to 1985. Bob Hesford
was one third of a classic Bristol back row,
combining his talents with those of Peter Polledri
and Mike Rafter. They were hugely influential as a
unit, never more so than in the 1983 cup final, in
which Hesford scored a try. Bob Hesford's father and
brother were professional goalkeepers, and another
brother was a leading Rugby League player. First
capped by England as a replacement against
Scotland in 1981, Bob Hesford won a total of
10 caps. He retired from playing in 1985 and later
became Bristol's coach.

R.J. Doubleday, a prop, provided a mobile but physical presence in the Bristol front row from 1976 to 1993. A farmer, John Doubleday went on England's 1979 tour to the Far East. He played in 3 Test matches but, as in the case of Nigel Pomphrey, was never awarded a full international cap. He sat on the bench for England during the 1979 international championship, and was capped at school, student and under-23 level. He was unusual in that he was equally at home playing on either side of the scrum. In a career plagued with injuries, John Doubleday played 314 games for Bristol and also represented Gloucestershire and the Barbarians.

John Doubleday's regular partner in the front row on many occasions was Austin Sheppard. A pupil with Alan Morley at Colston's School, and captain of the school XV, he joined Morley at the Memorial Ground from Old Colstonians in the 1973/74 season, initially as a second row. Briefly a member of Harlequins whilst doing an apprenticeship as a funeral director in London, Austin Sheppard made a total of 432 appearances for Bristol, finally retiring in 1989. He gained 2 England caps, making his debut as a replacement against Wales in 1981, and also appeared regularly for Gloucestershire and for divisional teams against touring sides.

Back-row forward, M.L. Baker, came comparatively late to first-class rugby, having played for local club Aretians for ten years, latterly as their captain. A product of Henbury Secondary School, Malcolm Baker started as a second-row forward, but was versatile enough to make occasional early appearances for Bristol United as a full-back. He made his Bristol debut in 1976 and, despite the presence of many other talented back-row players at the club throughout his career, he made a total of 234 first-team appearances, scoring 52 tries. Shown here in his England 'B' shirt, he scored a try on his England 'B' debut against Romania in 1978, and also played for Gloucestershire. An incredibly fit player, he made his final first-team appearance in 1988, and was still playing for Bristol United as recently as the 1993/94 season, by which time he was a Bristol committee-man.

K.M. Bogira formed, with Doubleday and Sheppard, Bristol's regular front row for many seasons. Of Polish descent, Kevin Bogira played his early rugby as a wing forward at Broad Plain, before joining Avonmouth Old Boys as a hooker in 1976. He later received valuable tuition from former Bristol hooker, John White, and made his Bristol debut in 1978. He was voted Player of the Year at the end of his first full season. In all, he made 317 appearances up to 1988, scoring 23 tries. He also played for Gloucestershire.

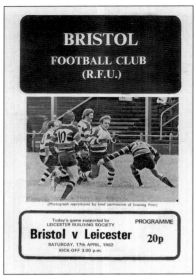

BRISTOL
FOOTBALL CLUB
(R.F.U.)

(Photograph reproduced by kind permission of Evening Post)

Today's game supported by
LEICESTER BUILDING SOCIETY

PROGRAMME

Bristol v Leicester   20p

SATURDAY, 17th APRIL, 1982
KICK-OFF 3.00 p.m.

1981/82 saw Bristol back to their best, under captain Alan Morley, with a final playing record of 35 wins and a draw from 44 matches. Once again, the team produced its best form following a cup disappointment – this time, a shock 12-10 home defeat against Liverpool. There were no more losses that season, and 14 consecutive wins included fine victories at Pontypool and Aberavon and a 38-4 demolition of Leicester. Bristol were never behind in any game of this winning run. This is the programme from the Leicester match.

R.A. Knibbs, a centre and one of Bristol's most charismatic players, made his debut as a seventeen-year-old against Pontypridd in 1982, scoring with his first touch of the ball. A player with an extraordinary repertoire of running angles, Ralph Knibbs scored many thrilling individual tries in a Bristol career which lasted until 1996. He played in the 1983 cup final as an eighteen year old, and represented Gloucestershire in all their games in the 1982/83 championship-winning campaign. He was also an accomplished basketball player, athlete and American football player. He played for the South West Division, England under-23s, and the England seven-a-side team, and made the admirable decision to turn down consideration for England's 1984 tour to South Africa, because of his opposition to apartheid. He also declared himself unavailable for England's 1988 tour to Australia, due to work commitments. Ralph Knibbs made 436 appearances for Bristol, scoring 123 tries, and was vice-captain during the centenary season. He later captained Clifton.

One of the all-time greats of Bristol rugby is flank forward, Mike Rafter. An inspirational leader, he played in 255 games between 1973 and 1985, captaining the club to victory in the 1983 cup final. He also had the distinction of captaining Gloucestershire to the county championship, three months earlier. Educated at St Brendan's College, he later studied physical education at St Luke's College, Exeter. Rafter's fearless work on the ground earned him the nickname 'Rafter the Grafter'. He played for England on 17 occasions, and was scandalously overlooked for the 1977 and 1980 British Lions tours. After injury forced his retirement, he coached at Bristol, Bedford and Bristol Combination club, St Mary's Old Boys. Perhaps it is not surprising that Mike Rafter was such an influential player: he is related to Sam Tucker, Bristol's greatest pre-war forward.

Despite being a dominant force in the game through much of the 1970s and early 1980s, Bristol had never enjoyed much luck in the cup. At last, in 1982/83, under Mike Rafter's captaincy, the team won the cup for the first and, to date, only time. However, Bristol had to negotiate a difficult hurdle in the semi-final – a trip to Coundon Road to face Coventry. Bristol's finest performance in reaching the cup final saw a stunning 23-3 victory, which included two glorious tries by Alan Morley. Here, the team is photographed before the match. From left to right, back row: I.H. Duggan, S.T. Hogg, R.A. Knibbs, P.J. Stiff, A.H. Troughton, A. Sheppard,R.J. Doubleday, J.F. Carr. Front row: R.J. Hesford, S. Barnes, P.J. Polledri, K.M. Bogira, M. Rafter (captain), A.J.G. Morley, L. Yandell.

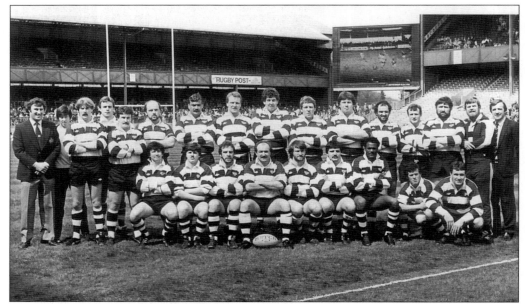

Bristol reached the 1983 final, despite being drawn away in every round, routine victories at Harrogate and Bedford being followed by a nail-biting quarter-final at West Hartlepool and the semi-final victory at Coventry. Here, the cup final squad line up at Twickenham, before their clash with Leicester. From left to right, back row: D.G. Tyler (coach), M. Lewis, D.P. Sorrell, I.H. Duggan, P.C. Cue, M. Tomlin, R.J. Hesford, N.J.C. Pomphrey, A.H. Troughton, R.J. Doubleday, P.J. Stiff, K.M. Bogira, D.J. Palmer, A. Sheppard, A.P. Ramsey, R. Reeves. Front row: R.M. Harding, S. Barnes, A.J.G. Morley, M. Rafter (captain), J.F. Carr, P.J. Polledri, R.A. Knibbs, L. Yandell, S.T. Hogg.

Bristol's 28-22 cup final victory over Leicester on a glorious late April afternoon, was considered at the time to be the best final yet staged. Trailing early in the game, the team eventually scored four tries, including two from left winger, John Carr, who had the distinction of scoring in every round. Both Bristol and Leicester played in lettered shirts, before professional rugby decreed otherwise. Before the 1983 cup final, selected Bristol players delighted their supporters by lining up to spell 'UP BRISTOL'. The 1983 cup final side was strong in all positions, and was superbly captained by Rafter. The arrival of outside half Stuart Barnes from Newport, was an important factor in the cup run. His goalkicking was invaluable in both the semi-final and the final itself.

Bristol's victory over Leicester was a great team effort. Stuart Barnes co-ordinated the moves and kicked his points, while the back row of Mike Rafter, Peter Polledri and Bob Hesford dominated the loose play. It was a magnificent game of rugby, played in front of a record 33,000 crowd, and Leicester contributed much to the spectacle. Here, Bristol skipper Mike Rafter celebrates victory by lifting the cup while Richard Harding and Bob Hesford savour the moment.

Stuart Barnes, an outside half, joined Bristol from Newport during the 1982/83 season, and scored 481 points in his 52 games for the club. Brought up in Wales, although born of English parents, he once held the record number of Welsh Schools' caps and was selected for the Welsh national squad in 1981, but switched allegiance to England. An Oxford blue, he made his England debut against Australia in 1984. He played for Bristol in the 1983 and 1984 cup finals and subsequently joined Bath in 1985. He won 10 caps for England in all. Stuart Barnes, who at one time trained with Cardiff City FC, toured New Zealand with the British Lions in 1993, and is now a broadcaster and writer on rugby.

1983/84, Mike Rafter's second season of captaincy, started badly with 10 defeats by the end of November. Thereafter, the old magic returned and only 4 further games were lost. Alas, one of these was the 1984 cup final, which Bristol lost 10-9 to neighbours, Bath. Barnes's kicking had got Bristol through a tight quarter-final at Waterloo, and a home semi-final against Harlequins, in which the visitors scored three tries to Bristol's one, but he missed a penalty with the final kick at Twickenham. For Bath, it was the start of an incredible run of cup final wins, and a lengthy dominance of West Country rugby. From left to right, back row: D.J. Hickey, P.J. Polledri, K.M. Bogira, R.J. Doubleday, N.J.C. Pomphrey. Middle row: S.T. Hogg, I.H. Duggan, D.L. Chidgey, R.A. Knibbs, P.J. Stiff, R.J. Hesford, D.J. Palmer, L. Yandell. Front row: J. Watson, J.F. Carr, P.C. Cue, A.J.G. Morley, M. Rafter (captain), A. Sheppard, S. Barnes.

J.F. Carr, initially a centre, made his name as a fast and powerful wing. Originally from the North East, John Carr joined Bristol during the 1980/81 season, and played for Gloucestershire whilst at Bristol University, later appearing in the 1983 championship-winning side. A prolific try scorer, he scored 42 tries in 51 Bristol appearances during the 1982/83 and 1983/84 seasons, and 127 in his 191 games for the club. His career was regularly interrupted by injuries, but he played for the England under-23 side and toured Japan with England Students. He also played in the South West Division's victory over Australia in 1988. Unlucky not to have had greater national recognition, he played with distinction on the wing, until a knee injury sustained at Leicester in March 1989 forced his retirement from competitive rugby.

Six
The Centenary
1984-1988

P.J. Polledri, a flank forward, was one of the greatest footballers to have played in the Bristol pack. A scrum-half at St Brendan's College, Peter Polledri won schoolboy caps for England, and later captained England under-23s. He deputized for the injured Richard Harding in the 1982/83 cup match at West Hartlepool, and helped to secure a famous win in that successful cup run. He captained Bristol from 1984 to 1986, and scored an impressive 84 tries in his 466 appearances for the club. After fifteen seasons with Bristol, he joined Clifton in 1990, and later coached them. Peter Polledri was one of Bristol's most creative and under-rated players.

The 1984/85 season, Peter Polledri's first as captain, saw Bristol winning 32 matches and scoring 1,036 points. Despite this success, the season was clouded by an emphatic 43-4 defeat at Leicester in the cup, although Bristol did manage a revenge victory at Welford Road later in the season. The club paid a visit to Germany at the end of September, where they defeated a Lower Saxony XV, 21-12. The game was arranged through the city of Bristol's close connections with Hanover. This is the official programme for the game.

1985/86 was a slightly disappointing season, during which 16 matches were lost, including all 8 played in Wales. The club gained unwanted world-wide publicity when playing Newport on 14 September 1985. Following a series of ugly incidents during the early part of the game, the referee, George Crawford of the London Society, took the unprecedented action of walking off. Local referee Paul Drake was at the ground and was called upon to continue the game, which Bristol won 21-14, without further incident. Subsequently, both clubs were reprimanded severely by their respective unions, and varying opinions were voiced over Mr Crawford's actions. This is the programme from the match.

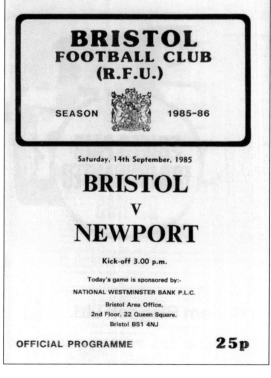

J.M. Webb, a full-back from Bristol University, was an outstanding attacking player, scoring 47 tries in his 122 games for Bristol. Jonathan Webb made his debut in the aforementioned match against Newport, and it was immediately apparent that Bristol had found a new star. His deceptive pace when coming into the line, together with his accomplished goal-kicking, were eventually recognized by England, and he made his international debut during the 1987 World Cup. He won 17 caps as a Bristol player, but, sadly, his form and confidence suffered as the club struggled to find a winning formula during the early days of league rugby. He left the club to join Bath, where he went on to become England's most-capped full-back, before retiring to follow a career in medicine.

T.W. Jones joined Bristol from Pontypool in 1951, when he took up a teaching post in the city. A wing or centre, Wynne Jones also played for Cardiff and Bedford, but once at Bristol, he devoted the majority of his playing career to the club. Wynne Jones played 54 games for the First XV and was a regular player with Bristol United, which he captained in the 1958/59 season. A Gloucestershire player on 13 occasions, he later played for Cleve. Wynne Jones served on the Bristol committee for several years and, following his retirement from teaching, he became the club's honorary secretary, a post he filled during the centenary season.

P.C. Cue, a fly-half or full-back, was a popular Bristol player, frequently thrilling the crowds with his jinking runs and clever kicks. A talented all-round sportsman, Phil Cue had two soccer trials for Aston Villa whilst at Patchway High School, and also excelled at cricket, basketball and athletics. In all, he made 274 Bristol first-team appearances, scoring 759 points. He also represented England under-23s and Gloucestershire. When county rugby was spurned by the senior clubs in the mid-1980s, Phil Cue chose to continue playing for Gloucestershire. This lost him his Bristol first-team place, and he eventually joined Bath. He later played for Clifton.

Nigel Pomphrey took over as captain for the 1986/87 season, during which only 12 games were lost and 1,204 points scored. Bristol returned to winning ways in Wales, defeating South Wales Police on 22 November, and then caused a sensation by defeating Llanelli (28-6) at Stradey Park in December. It was Bristol's first victory at Llanelli for ten years, and gave them a rare double over the Scarlets, following an earlier 18-3 win at Bristol. This is the programme for Bristol's win at Llanelli.

In 1987/88, the club celebrated its centenary. After an uncertain beginning, which saw 3 defeats in the first 6 games, Bristol struck a rich vein of form, winning 21 consecutive matches. This run included away wins at Gloucester and Cardiff, and at Kelso and Selkirk on the centenary tour to Scotland. The club peaked in a memorable cup semi-final victory, 34-6 at Moseley, but were unable to crown the season by winning the cup. They lost to Harlequins in an exciting final, 28-22, and were defeated by the same opponents a week later in an equally thrilling Middlesex Sevens final. The illustration shows the cup final programme.

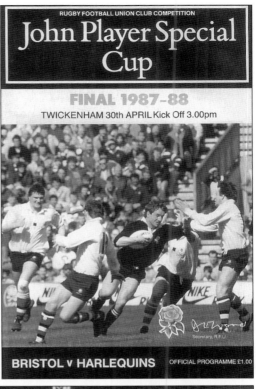

The club came up with the inspired idea of reverting to the original colours of slate, yellow and brown for some of the centenary matches. These colours, last used in 1891, were worn for the first home game of the season, appropriately against Cardiff, Bristol's first ever opponents. Unfortunately, Cardiff spoilt the party by winning 20-15. The photograph shows Bristol number eight forward, Geoff Crane, with the ball, closely supported by centenary captain Nigel Pomphrey (left) and second row, Matthew Skuse (right).

Another special centenary event saw the reunion of many former captains of the club. This occasion was staged at the Mansion House in Clifton, by invitation of the Lord Mayor. Down the stairs from the back: Nigel Pomphrey, Alan Morley, Peter Polledri, Mike Rafter, Mike Fry, Dave Rollitt, Ken Plummer, Tony Nicholls, Dave Tyler, Bill Redwood, Derek Neate, Peter Colston, Dick Hawkes, Bert Macdonald, Doug Pratten. Front row: Bill Woodward, Vic Thompson, Harry Sherman, Jack Gregory, George Gibbs, Tom Mahoney (centenary president).

The Bristol club was formed at a meeting in the Montpelier Hotel on 11 April 1888, and the club commemorated this occasion by restaging it a century later. Here, Bristol committee-men Arnold Johnson, Wynne Jones and Tom Mahoney listen, while suitably-dressed local actors re-enact the meeting. On show are various items of club memorabilia.

Bristol's special centenary match against the world-famous invitation club, the Barbarians, was played on 21 October 1987. Bristol appeared to be heading for defeat in this game, as full time approached, but two late tries earned them a 20-20 draw. The teams were photographed together before the match.

This picture shows Bristol's centenary season committee. Committees, such as this one, have devoted countless hours of unpaid time to the club throughout its history, and this picture includes many who served Bristol over a considerable number of years. Amongst those shown, are Eric Blackman (a scrum-half during the Blake era, who has done much to promote schools' rugby in the Bristol area), Reg Brookes (another member with strong schools' connections), and Ken Coggins (who, as well as working tirelessly for junior rugby, has preserved many items relating to the club's history). From left to right, back row: Malcolm Baker, John Watson, Ron Mayo, Arthur Holmes, Ken Coggins, Gordon Lovell, Dennis Skinner, Mike Blackmore, Derek Neate, Richard Cecil, Jack Palmer, Sid Kemp, Alan Morley. Front row: Bill Redwood, Reg Brookes, Wynne Jones, Nigel Pomphrey, Eric Blackman, Tom Mahoney, Alan Ramsey, Jock Wilson, David Taylor, John Marsh, David Whittle.

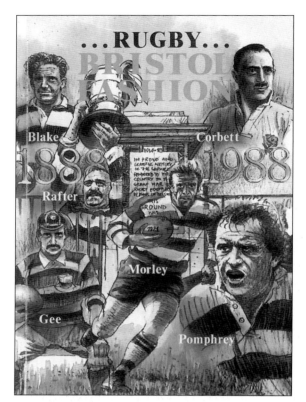

Local rugby journalist, Chris Ducker, was invited to write the club's centenary book, appropriately entitled *Rugby Bristol Fashion*. It featured an attractive cover illustration by Frank Dougherty, showing Bristol captains of various eras.

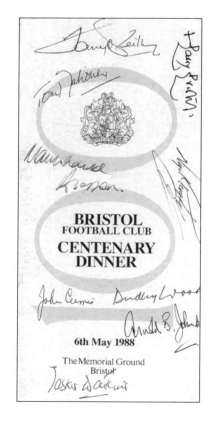

The centenary season culminated in a magnificent club dinner held in a marquee on the Memorial Ground. Over 900 guests attended this event, and enjoyed a brilliant speech by Bristol's old friend, Tony O'Reilly. This is the menu for the occasion, signed by centenary captain, Nigel Pomphrey, and various special guests, including O'Reilly himself, the Lord Mayor, and the Bishop of Bristol.

T.A.B. Mahoney first played for Bristol in 1936, and made the last of his 84 first-team appearances during the 1949/50 season. Tom Mahoney was educated at local rugby stronghold, St Brendan's College, and joined Bristol from Old Redcliffians. A hard-working forward, he also played many games for Bristol United, and captained them for three seasons. Tom Mahoney went on to become one of the club's most loyal and industrious officials. Following a lengthy spell as First XV secretary, he was appointed honorary general secretary of the club in 1966, and retired from this office in 1987, whereupon he was made centenary season president. A truly devoted clubman, Tom Mahoney was deservedly awarded the MBE in 1994 for services to the game.

During the centenary season, the club launched an appeal for £500,000, with the aim of building a new stand on the eastern side of the Memorial Ground. This was duly completed by the start of the following season, but the project was dogged by misfortune. Amongst other problems, sections of the pitch could not be seen from certain seats, and many supporters were sorry to see the demolition of the popular terrace shed. Eventually, Bristol refused to pay the final bill on the stand, and won a legal action over this. The photograph shows Bristol centenary president, Tom Mahoney, cutting the first sod, watched by other members of the committee.

S.T. Hogg, usually a centre or outside half, joined Bristol from Exeter University in 1982, having previously attended Bristol Grammar School. A regular goal kicker with the club, Simon Hogg notched up 1,033 points during his ten years at the Memorial Ground, including 45 tries. He played for Devon when at college, and later represented Gloucestershire. At the start of the centenary season, he was playing with local club Old Bristolians, but was recalled to Bristol and played at fly-half in the Barbarians match. He went on to be a major factor in Bristol's success during the season. Simon Hogg, very much a Corinthian in his approach to the game, played a total of 222 matches for Bristol, and later played for Clifton. He played for England under-23s and England Students, and appeared in all three of Bristol's cup finals during the 1980s.

A.F. Dun, who succeeded Nigel Pomphrey as captain in 1988/89, was a team-mate of Simon Hogg at Bristol Grammar School, before continuing his education at St Bartholomew's Hospital in London. Andy Dun toured Australia and New Zealand with England Schools in 1979, and also played for England under-23s and England Students, captaining both sides. He gained his solitary England cap as a Wasps player in the 1984 game against Wales. Andy Dun, who captained Wasps as well as Bristol, played 170 Bristol matches, scoring 39 tries.

Seven
Leagues and Professionalism
1988-2001

Following experiments with merit tables, league rugby was introduced into the English game in 1987. Bristol had difficulty coming to terms with the demands of the new system, and rarely achieved consistency in league games. During the following season Bristol could only finish seventh in the league, and lost to a last-minute score in a cup quarter-final at Bath, played in monsoon conditions. This is the 1988/89 team, from left to right, back row: P.J. Polledri, R.A. Knibbs, A.G. Blackmore, P.J. Stiff, G. Crane. Middle row: E.J. Blackman (chairman), B. Whitehead, P. Jeffrey, D.J. Eves, P. Collings, P. Smith, M. Tainton, J.F. Carr, S. Painter, A. Saxby, J.S. Marsh (treasurer), D.J. Skinner, T.W. Jones (secretary). Front row: J. Biggins, M. Cotton, R.M. Harding, I.H. Duggan, A.F. Dun (captain), T.A.B. Mahoney (president), A.V. Sharp, R.J. Doubleday, D. Palmer, A.E. Ramsey.

John Watson, a centre, was one of the most loyal and dedicated players to have worn the Bristol jersey. He played for the First XV in 204 games from 1978 to 1990, and crossed for 32 tries. He was captain of the successful Bristol United teams of 1986/87 and 1987/88, when the team won 54 of their 71 games. In 1988/89, Bristol decided to introduce a Third XV, the first time this venture had been tried since the early years of the club. John Watson was appointed as the first captain of this team, known as Bristol 'A' XV. The 'A' XV's first season was very successful, with only 2 games being lost out of 33, and over 1,000 points being scored.

Friendly matches continued during the early years of the league, and Bristol often played their most attractive rugby during these games. In 1988/89, Bristol defeated Cardiff twice in a season, for the first time since 1930/31. Bristol won an exciting game at Cardiff in September (23-17) and then completed the double with a home victory (20-12) the following March. This is the programme for the home match.

1989/90 was a disappointing season. The club found itself, briefly, at the top of the league after winning its first 3 games, but no further league games were won until the last game of the season. Bristol had an exciting pair of wingers in Frenchman Eric Thillet, and Barry Whitehead, whose eventual career total of tries was 46 in 63 matches, but, once again, the best rugby was played in friendly matches. This is the programme for Bristol's 58-4 victory at Rugby in December 1989.

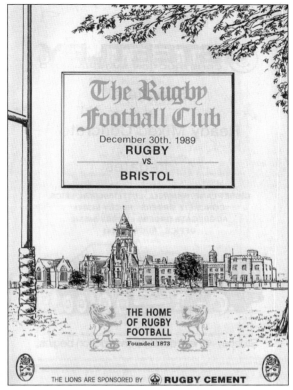

P. Collings, a back-row forward, played for Bristol from 1986 to 1992. An athletic player, Paul Collings scored 70 tries in his 179 games, and would have played in many more matches for Bristol, had it not been for a series of injuries that plagued him. Formerly with Old Redcliffians, Collings was capped by England at schoolboy level. He played in the 1988 cup final and was in the Bristol team that narrowly lost the final of the Middlesex Sevens the following weekend. He was Bristol's leading try scorer in 1988/89, and was joint top the following season. Forced to retire prematurely from rugby, Paul Collings now lives in Australia.

P.J. Stiff, a lock and prop, played 360 games for Bristol between 1978 and 1995, and was a great favourite with supporters. Peter Stiff, who joined the club from Bristol Harlequins, formed a powerful second-row partnership with Nigel Pomphrey in the early 1980s. A feature of his game were his powerful runs from tapped penalties, a set move also perfected by Pomphrey and one which wreaked havoc in defences, frequently leading to tries. Stiff crossed for 85 tries for Bristol. He was later tried as a tight-head prop, and represented the England 'B' side in this position, but the change wasn't entirely successful. An occasional goal kicker, Peter Stiff was appointed captain of Bristol United for the 1991/92 season, and ended up making 35 first-team appearances, being voted supporters' Player of the Year.

D.J. Palmer succeeded Kevin Bogira as Bristol's regular hooker, and made 263 appearances in a career lasting from 1981 to 1994. Educated at Monks Park School, David Palmer played for Old Redcliffians, but came to Bristol's notice as a member of the highly successful Bristol Colts XV. He replaced the injured Bogira during the 1983 cup final, and went on to play in Bristol's losing finals of 1984 and 1988. He also played for the South West against Australia in 1984.

Giant Bristolian lock, A.G. Blackmore, dominated the Bristol line-out for eleven seasons, following his debut in 1984. Curiously, he made his Gloucestershire county debut before he played for Bristol. Andy Blackmore was an outstanding athlete, who represented the England Schools' team at basketball. He was selected for England under-23s and, on one occasion, when chosen as a replacement at this level, was asked to play for their opponents, an England Students' XV. He regularly played for England 'A', and was unlucky not to be selected for England's tour to South Africa in 1994. He was one of many Bristol players who were close to full inter-national honours, without receiving a well-deserved call up. Andy Blackmore played 251 games for Bristol and, subse-quently, played for Coventry and Clifton. He later became a rugby development officer for the Rugby Football Union.

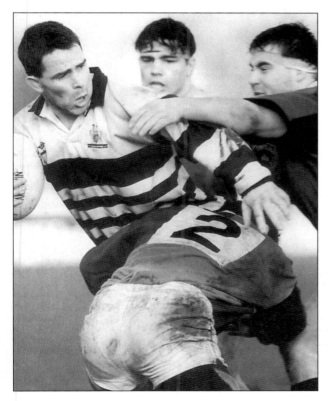

D.J. Eves started his playing career at the club as a colt, and captained the colts team in 1983/84 and 1984/85. A flanker, Derek Eves was appointed Bristol captain for the 1990/91 season, and remained in charge for five seasons, a record equalled only by J.W. Jarman, back in the early years of the club. Renowned for his speed and leader-ship skills, he played for England Colts, the England Sevens squad, Emerging England, England 'A', and the Barbarians. He left the Bristol club in 1995 to play for Coventry, where he also acted as coaching administrator. He returned to Bristol during their season in Allied Dunbar Premiership Two in 1998/99, and played an important role in inspiring the team to the championship during the final weeks of the season. Derek Eves played 278 games for Bristol, scoring 88 tries, and played 93 games for Bristol United.

For the 1990/91 season, the club decided to appoint a professional director of coaching. The man selected was Colin McFadyean, briefly a Bristol player in his early playing days, and later an England centre and a 1966 British Lion. Bristol had an indifferent season, and were threatened with relegation, pulling themselves clear of danger thanks only to late-season home wins over Gloucester and Leicester, and a draw at Moseley, McFadyean's old club. At the end of the season, McFadyean, pictured here in his playing days, left the club, and Bristol decided to appoint former captain, David Tyler, as club administrator.

Mark Tainton, an outside half, joined Bristol from local club, Cleve, in 1981, and made 240 appearances for the first team from 1984 to 1997. His career total of 2063 points is a club record, beating Alan Pearn's total of 2,047. An England Colts player, Mark Tainton was appointed as coach of Bristol's backs for the 2000/01 season, and has also been in demand as a kicking coach. His career totals of 416 conversions and 366 penalties are also Bristol records.

Prop forward, A.V. Sharp, earned Schools' and England 'B' caps, before gaining 6 caps for Scotland. Educated at St Brendan's College, Alan Sharp was the cornerstone of the Bristol scrum in 171 games. An abrasive customer, he relished the physical encounters provided by league rugby. He first played for Bristol in 1987, after playing for St Brendan's Old Boys. He left Bristol in the early 1990s, and played for Clifton and Coventry, but returned and added valuable skill and experience to the team which strove to gain promotion from the Second Division during the 1998/99 season. Injuries regularly interrupted his career and he played his last game during the 1999/2000 season.

1991/92 was an inconsistent season for Bristol, during which a policy was developed of fielding weakened teams for non-league matches. This resulted in Bristol losing to Clifton for the first time since 1954, a victory which Clifton repeated later in the season against another under-strength team. Bristol finished tenth in the league, and used a total of 63 players in all their games. One of the few highlights was an impressive 32-0 league victory at Nottingham in November. The illustration shows the programme from the game.

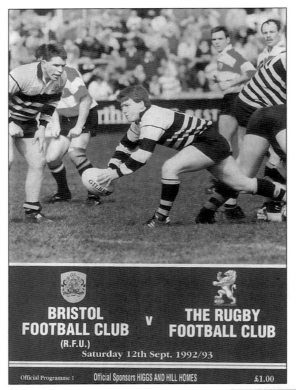

1992/93 was a much better season, which saw Bristol rise to sixth in the league. There was also much more success in friendly matches, including exciting wins at Cardiff and Bridgend. This was the season in which the club, under the guidance of local journalist John Harding, revolutionized the design and content of the match programme, setting a standard for other clubs to emulate. This is the first issue of the new-look programme for Bristol's 35-13 victory over Rugby.

K.P.P. Bracken, a scrum-half, joined Bristol whilst a student at Bristol University. Kyran Bracken represented Waterloo, Lancashire, and England Schools' teams as an outside half, before becoming a scrum-half and captaining the England 18-group Schools side. He made a celebrated debut for England in the defeat of New Zealand in 1993. He joined Saracens at the end of the 1995/96 season, having played 61 games and scored 17 tries for Bristol. He later captained England, and accompanied Bristol colleagues Mark Regan and Simon Shaw on the 1997 British Lions tour to South Africa, as a replacement.

In 1993/94, for the first time, league fixtures were played on a home and away basis, and Bristol enjoyed their best league season to date, finishing fourth. The season was a personal triumph for skipper, Derek Eves, who captained England Emerging Players, and was selected for the Barbarians. At the end of the season, the club won the National Tens, a short-lived competition which was staged at Gloucester. Bristol defeated the host club in the final. This is the tournament programme.

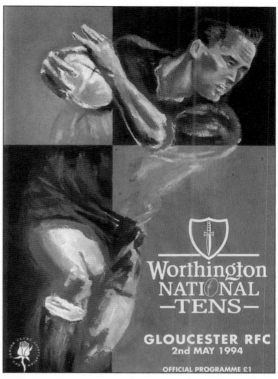

Bristol returned to their inconsistent ways during the 1994/95 season, finishing only sixth in the league, despite a promising start, which included a narrow victory at Northampton. The club experienced a shock 47-11 defeat at West Hartlepool in October, but bounced back the following week to defeat Leicester 31-22. They also gained a badly-needed 10-9 win at Harlequins in February. This is the match programme. At the end of the season, the club decided to register under the Industrial and Provident Societies Acts, and became Bristol Football Club Ltd. Events in the subsequent close season, meant that 1994/95 was to be the final season of amateur rugby for Bristol.

119

BRISTOL
FOOTBALL CLUB
—— RFU ——
CELEBRATION
DINNER

of

Paul Hull's

**England Tour to
South Africa**

Summer 1994

**Forte Crest Hotel
Bristol**

**Thursday, 15th September,
1994**

P.A. Hull, a full-back, was one of Bristol's most potent attackers in a career which extended from 1987 to 2000. Possessing blistering pace and remarkable footballing skills, Paul Hull was one of the most popular players of the 1990s. He joined Bristol when posted to RAF Lyneham, and later became captain for the 1995/96 season. He was capped by England on 4 occasions in 1994. A physical training instructor in the Royal Air Force, he regularly played for Combined Services teams against touring sides. Good enough to play anywhere in the three-quarters, he played regularly at outside half when the club needed him to do so. Hull scored 61 tries for Bristol and was an accomplished goal kicker, scoring 368 points with the boot. A Barbarian, Paul Hull retired during the 1999/2000 season, and took control of Bristol's successful under-21 squad. Bristol staged a dinner in honour of Paul Hull's England tour, and the illustration shows the menu from this event.

Hooker M.P. Regan made his Bristol debut in 1991, having served his apprenticeship with Bristol Colts under Bristol's inspirational Colts coach, Elwyn Price. Mark Regan first played rugby as a schoolboy at Keynsham, then St Bernadette's, before attending St Brendan's College. He was capped by England at Schools' level, and earned the first of the 13 full caps he won from Bristol, in the first England international of the professional era against South Africa in 1995. He was selected for the 1997 British Lions tour to South Africa, and played in the final test. He joined Bath on his return. Mark Regan played 120 games for Bristol and also represented Gloucestershire.

Rugby was declared a professional game following the 1995 World Cup, and Bristol struggled to adapt to the demands of the new era. There was a tense end to the 1995/96 season, with Bristol needing to beat Saracens at the Memorial Ground to avoid possible relegation. They retained their place in the top division with a 21-7 win, and eventually finished sixth. Here, hooker, Mark Regan, controls the ball, before delivering it to scrum-half, Kyran Bracken. Behind Regan, is lock, G.S. Archer. Army officer Garath Archer, joined Bristol in 1994 and was capped by England in 1996. He returned to his home club Newcastle at the end of the 1995/96 season, before rejoining Bristol in 1999/2000.

S.D. Shaw, a 6ft 9in second row, was one of the biggest forwards ever to have worn a Bristol shirt. Simon Shaw was the uncapped player in the Barbarians side which defeated South Africa in 1994, but a broken ankle in Bristol's 1995 game against Transvaal delayed his international debut. He subsequently gained 6 England caps as a Bristol player. He made his Bristol debut in 1992, but joined Wasps at the end of the 1996/97 season, after 93 appearances. Simon Shaw toured with the British Lions in South Africa in 1997.

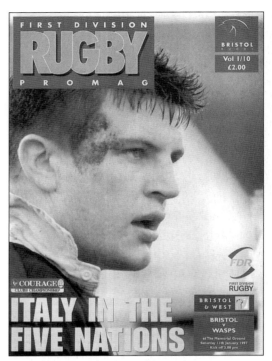

At the start of the 1996/97 season Bristol Rovers FC were invited to share the Memorial Ground facilities. Bristol were coached by former Wales coach, Alan Davies, but, despite his pedigree, Bristol struggled to cope with the pace and power of the other sides in the division. It was a disjointed season and, although the team looked good on paper, they failed to gel as a unit and were unsuccessful on the pitch. Despite being well led by back-row forward, Martin Corry, Bristol had to defeat Bedford, National League Two champions, in home and away play-offs, to remain in the top division. Bristol won both games. Corry, shown here on the front of a Bristol home programme, was capped by England on their Argentinian tour at the end of the season, but then joined Leicester, after 48 appearances. He became a British Lion in 2001.

This photograph shows action from Bristol's first home game from 1996/97, a 38-10 victory over Orrell. Here, scrum-half Robert Jones clears the ball from a ruck. Jones, a former British Lion and captain of Wales, played 50 games for the club, captaining Bristol the following season. The other Bristol players are Eben Rollitt (on the ground), David Corkery (with the scrum cap), Phil Adams (with foot raised), Simon Shaw (behind) and Kris Fullman (extreme right). Phil 'Grizzly' Adams, a second row, played in 195 first-team games in his twelve seasons with Bristol. After he retired, in 1998, he became team manager, and still works for the Bristol club.

With the establishment of separate English and Welsh leagues, Bristol's only opportunities to play Welsh clubs now came through European tournaments. Here, six Bristol forwards await an attempt at goal at a sunny Ebbw Vale in September 1997. From left to right: Kevin Dunn (hooker), Kris Fullman (prop), Ritchie Collins (loose forward), John Wakeford and Chad Eagle (locks), and David Corkery (wing forward). Collins and Wakeford had previously been capped by Wales, and, along with Dunn, joined Bristol in the autumn of their careers. Corkery was a fine forward, capped 25 times by Ireland. He was the star in a pack which struggled to come to terms with most of their opponents during the season.

The 1997/98 season was a disaster. Under the captaincy of Robert Jones, only 2 league games were won, and Bristol received some dreadful hammerings, most notably a 76-0 humiliation at Sale. An incredible 40-38 victory at Harlequins briefly raised spirits, but Bristol were bundled out of the cup by lowly Worcester, and coach Alan Davies was sacked. The end result was another appearance in the play-offs and, although Bristol looked to have done a reasonable damage-limitation exercise in restricting opponents London Scottish to a 29-25 win in the first leg, nothing went right in the home leg, which was lost 17-15. This is the programme from that fateful day, which saw Bristol relegated.

The ensuing summer was one of high emotion and suspense for all who cared about the club. Chairman Arthur Holmes, who had so often rescued Bristol with financial help, decided to put the club into administration. To make matters worse, a clause in the ground-sharing agreement allowed Bristol Rovers to buy the Memorial Ground, by purchasing Bristol's share for a mere £10,000. For a while, it appeared that the club had breathed its last. Enter local businessman Malcolm Pearce, pictured, with an eleventh-hour rescue package. Unlike many entrepreneurs who had speculated in professional rugby, Pearce genuinely loved the game. A new company, Bristol Rugby Ltd, was established and the club was able to take its place in Allied Dunbar Premiership Two, albeit as tenants at the renamed Memorial Stadium.

On reflection, relegation proved a blessing in disguise. Despite the disappearance of many top players, Malcolm Pearce was able to recruit Bob Dwyer, the former Australian national coach. Dwyer had only three weeks to assemble and train his squad, but a new-look side won its first game, at Exeter, 22-15. What followed was, for many, a golden season, with visits to new venues such as Wakefield and Rotherham, coupled with nostalgic returns to old friends, such as Waterloo and London Welsh. This picture from the London Welsh game shows a group of Bristol forwards during a pause in play. From left to right: Al Charron (a Canadian international, who became Player of the Year), Dawson Tamati, Chad Eagle, Alan Sharp.

Bristol used 44 players during the 1998/99 league campaign, many of whom became firm favourites with the club's supporters. Besides Al Charon, other popular players were Australian forward, Mark Gabey, Hong Kong international winger, Luke Nabaro, and future New Zealand All Black, Mark Robinson. The defining moment in a nail-biting climax to the season was Robinson's amazing 50-metre try in the seventh minute of injury time, to secure a 43-39 victory at Fylde. Robinson is shown here on the cover of Bristol's final home programme of the season.

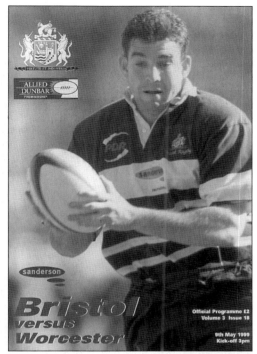

Despite the close attentions of Worcester and Rotherham, Bristol reached their final game needing to defeat Worcester at home to achieve promotion and win the league. The game itself was a tense encounter, which Bristol won 21-11. This gave them the league title by a points difference of ten over Rotherham. Here, the team celebrate Bristol's return to top-flight rugby.

Bristol's first season back in the top flight saw the arrival of many new players, including South African fly-half, Henry Honiball, Argentinian scrum-half, Agustin Pichot, and, briefly, veteran New Zealand centre, Frank Bunce. The new captain was former England number eight, Dean Ryan. A more than satisfactory season saw Bristol finish sixth in the league and reach two semi-finals. This is the programme for Bristol's European Shield semi-final against Pau, which was played at Tarbes. Bristol reached this stage of the competition by defeating Biarritz away in the quarter-final, despite fielding an under-strength side, but Pau won the semi-final, 51-27, and went on to defeat Castres in the final.

Bristol's other semi-final was in the Tetley's Bitter Cup. In a bizarre game at the Madejski Stadium in Reading they lost 44-31 to Wasps, despite scoring five tries in the last twenty minutes. Here, Bristol's multi-national front row of Pablo Lemoine, Barry Williams and Paul Johnstone, await the feed from Agustin Pichot. Lemoine, a Uruguayan who played in the 1999 World Cup, was a hugely popular player with the Bristol crowd. He played 44 games for Bristol and scored 3 tries. Williams, a Welsh international and 1997 British Lion, was a mobile hooker, who scored 16 tries during his 51 games for the club. Johnstone, a Zimbabwean test prop with Scottish qualifications, proved a tough forward and the cornerstone of the Bristol pack, and by the end of the 2000/2001 season he had crossed for 10 tries in his 56 games.

Bob Dwyer returned to Australia to coach New South Wales before the start of the 2000/2001 season, and Dean Ryan took over as coach. In a disappointing season, 5 of the first 6 games were lost, and there were only 3 away victories. The 2000/01 squad, from left to right, back row: A. Sheridan, S. Nelson, D.L. Rees, L. Best, G.S. Archer, S. Morgan, C. Short, J. Ogilvie-Bull, J. Mayer, A. M. Bennett, M. McCarrick. Middle row: P.A. Hull, M. Tainton, M. Salter, S. Vile, B. Sturnham, S. Brown, K. Fullman, E. Simone, A. Cadwallader, A. Brown, D. Crompton, R. Siveter, S. Fenn, Donna Sanderson, P. Johnstone, K. James, E. Hanley, L.B. Davies. Front row: O. Booyse, N. McCarthy, J. Brownrigg, D. Dewdney, G. Bowen, L. Nabaro, D. Ryan, A. Pichot (captain), B. Williams, G. Baber, L. Gerrard, A. Vander, S. Marsden, M. Evans.

During the professional era, all leading English clubs have relied greatly on imported foreign players. Agustin Pichot was appointed Bristol captain for the 2000/01 season, and was joined by fellow Argentine international, Felipe Contepomi, to form a successful half-back partnership. During this season, Pichot played for the Barbarians against South Africa, but injury sustained in that match ruled him out of selection and affected his form. Bristol were fortunate that, in Gareth Baber, they had a player of considerable ability to step in, both as scrum-half and captain. Contepomi offered a physical alternative at outside half, as well as being an outstanding goal kicker. On 2 December 2000, Bristol defeated Bath for the first time in the league. Here, Pichot (right) and Contepomi celebrate the 16-9 victory. It was a game in which Pichot scored the only try and Contepomi kicked eleven points.

Besides the defeat of Bath, Bristol did well to beat eventual champions Leicester, and produced some superb rugby on the final day of the season, when Northampton were beaten 46-16. This photograph, from Bristol's drawn game at London Irish, shows scrum-capped forwards, Garath Archer, Alex Brown and Paul Johnstone with London Irish hooker, Richard Kirke. Archer and Brown were Bristol's first-choice locks, with Brown winning the Player of the Year award for his outstanding line-out work. He was rewarded with selection for England's tour to North America at the end of the season.

Under-21 rugby has taken on an increasingly high profile in recent years, and Bristol have been at the forefront of the game at this level. Coach Paul Hull has ensured the achievement of one of Malcolm Pearce's main objectives, namely the development of local rugby talent. Here, the under-21 squad celebrate their second consecutive league title, following their 36-24 victory over Bath in April 2001. The team was undefeated all season and, if these talented players can make a successful transition to senior rugby, the future looks bright for Bristol.